A DEACON'S HEART

A DEACON'S HEART

The New United Methodist Diaconate

Margaret Ann Crain
and
Jack L. Seymour

With Jimmy Carr
and
Joaquín García

ABINGDON PRESS
Nashville

A DEACON'S HEART:
THE NEW UNITED METHODIST DIACONATE

Copyright © 2001 by Abingdon Press

This book is printed on recycled, acid-free paper.

ISBN 978-0-687-09032-7

Cataloging-in-Publication Data is available from the Library of Congress.

Scripture quotations, unless otherwise indicated, are from the New Revised Standard Version Bible, copyright © 1989, by the Division of Christian Education of the National Council of the Churches of Christ in the United States of America.

Scripture quotations marked (CEV) are from the Contemporary English Version Copyright © 1991, 1992, 1995 by American Bible Society. Used by permission.

Scripture quotations noted RSV are from the Revised Standard Version of the Bible, copyright 1946, 1952, 1971 by the Division of Christian Education of the National Council of Churches of Christ in the USA. Used by permission.

Quotations marked *1996 BOD* are taken from *The United Methodist Book of Discipline 1996* © 1996 by The United Methodist Publishing House. Used by permission.

01 02 03 04 05 06 07 08 09 10—10 9 8 7 6 5 4 3 2 1

MANUFACTURED IN THE UNITED STATES OF AMERICA

To our colleagues at Garrett-Evangelical
Theological Seminary:
a community of faith and learning
open to the whole people of God

CONTENTS

FOREWORD

A Deacon's Heart is a significant gift not only to The United Methodist Church but also to the larger ecumenical community. The diaconate is growing at a tremendous pace in many denominations around the world. In all communions that have chosen to establish a permanent diaconate, emphasis has been exerted in interpreting the meaning and influence of the new orders and offices to the total ministry of the Church.

This book will take its place as an interpretive resource on the new deacon in The United Methodist Church. It will assist in understanding not only the vision of the deacon, but how the very nature of the diaconate can lead the Church in renewal.

It is important to note that Margaret Ann Crain is a deacon in full connection and Jack Seymour is an elder in full connection in The United Methodist Church. They bring to the discussion not only understanding of ministry from two different orders, but also from their broad experiences in the Church. Both have been committed to a stronger and more significant role of the community of faith in bringing healing to a broken world. Their insights on the ministry of the deacon are strongly influenced by their personal commitments to Christian education that equips and leads the baptized to be God's servants wherever their daily lives may take them.

Margaret Ann Crain and Jack Seymour's research has provided a concrete glimpse into the life and work of deacons. They have documented on behalf of deacons the commitment to and the practice of linking worship and work that will greatly enhance the broader Church in its ministry. Through the stories of deacons, the Church can visualize how the deacon can lead as a missional office in individual ministries of love, justice, and service while assisting all Christians in claiming their ministries.

Crain and Seymour assist the reader in seeing, with new glasses, the beginnings of orders in the life of the Church. The reality that the "divisions of labor" in the early Church grew out of the eucharistic meal not only helped the community to function smoothly but also brought a commitment to healing God's broken creation. It is a reminder that all in the community of faith have a responsibility in this work of reconciliation based on the needs of the people.

The calling of the deacon to meet the needs of the world is historically grounded through predecessor diaconate offices in the Church. This calling from God to lead in the healing of creation provides new missional focus for the Church. The basis of all ministry is to bring wholeness to brokenness, suffering, and oppression, thus claiming the harmony intended by God for all people and things.

New insight into the sacramental nature of the deacon is shared in this book. The deacon as defined by The United Methodist Church has one foot in the Church and one foot in the world thus creating a bridge between worship and work. The authors suggest that the deacon is testimony to the sacramental nature of all creation. All acts of love and justice point to God's presence everywhere and in everyone. Deacons are responsible for seeing that the community is faithful in sharing the gifts of love to all. This bridge ministry of the deacon does not take away the ministry of the laity. On the contrary, it exists to make more effective the ministry of all Christians. As Crain and Seymour state so well, "Deacons will fail in being God's instruments if they are the only ones that do the work. Deacons must claim their responsibility of equipping the saints for more effective daily ministries."

This book certainly does not have all the answers but it makes concrete suggestions on the nature and work of the "new old" Order of Deacons in relation to practices in The United Methodist Church. The authors have shared new insights and raised significant questions regarding the practice of ministry of the deacon. They have led to the edge of our understanding and knowledge with suggestions and asked "What now?" The contribution of this book will be of great value as the Church discerns the new roles of not only the Order of Deacons but also the Order of Elders and the ministry of the laity.

—JIMMY CARR
Former Assistant General Secretary
Division of Ordained Ministry
Section of Deacons and Diaconal Ministries
General Board of Higher Education and Ministry
The United Methodist Church

—JOAQUÍN GARCÍA
Assistant General Secretary
Division of Ordained Ministry
Section of Deacons and Diaconal Ministries
General Board of Higher Education and Ministry
The United Methodist Church

ACKNOWLEDGMENTS

The writing of this book has been a communal effort. We thank those who have shared convictions, questions, and stories with us as we have explored together the meaning of servant ministry, ordination, and call. We thank our colleagues (faculty, administration, and students) at Garrett-Evangelical who are seeking to build a community of faith and learning that is open to the whole people of God. For the vision of spiritual leadership that guides faculty reflection, we thank President Neal Fisher. "To know God in Christ, and through preparing spiritual leaders, to assist others to know God in Christ," the seminary's core purpose, is a call to the whole people of God and an invitation to mutuality and partnership. We name our colleagues Dwight and Linda Vogel, George Kalantzis, and Ed Phillips who have read sections of this manuscript, asked questions, and offered directions. We also thank "Deacons: In His Service," a student group at Garrett-Evangelical, whose experiences and probing questions have found their way into the manuscript.

We particularly appreciate the assistance given by the staff of the Division of Ordained Ministry, Section of Deacons and Diaconal Ministries, General Board of Higher Education and Ministry of The United Methodist Church, who have provided support and encouragement. Jimmy Carr, Paul Van Buren, and Joaquín García have read sections of the manuscript and offered important suggestions.

Most of all, we thank those who have shared their

stories with us and without whose voice and commitment this book could not have been written. Some of those who shared their lives with us include: Pam Auble, Alan Benson, Shay Blackwell, Rosalee Blake, Liv Berit Carlsen, Joy Carr, JoAnne Chase, Ula Christopher, Marie Clark, Dottie Davis Clarke, Rosemary Davis, Regina Davis-Bridges, Kay DeMoss, David Dodge, Don and Marjean Ehlers, Clara Ester, Linda Evans, Deborah Burns Fox, Nancy Gable, Donna Gaither, Terry Gladstone, Raney Good, Kathy Harrington-Tabor, Jim Harvey, Betsey Heavner, Denise Hage, Mary Hedgecock, Jeanne Higgins, Carol Hoffman-Guzman, Ellen Hopkins, Adrienne Ann Ilseman, Donna Inman, Olive Long Kellum, Carol Krau, Daniel B. Lee, Julie Hager Love, Sondra Matthaei, Joy and David Melton, Patty Meyers, Becky Michael, Mary Elizabeth Moore, Margaret Moyer, Nick Nicholas, Melissa Nichols, Diane Olson, Matthew Packer, MaryJane Pierce-Norton, Elizabeth Box Price, Jo Ross, Sharon Rubey, Ken Runkle, Sandra Sagehorn, Andrew Schleicher, Patti Smith, Deanna Stickley-Miner, Joyce Sluss, Jim Tice, Virginia Tinsley, Linda Vogel, Karen Warren, Lynne Westfield, Susan Wilhauck, Margaret Ann Williams, Sally Wizik Wills, Betsy Youdris, Nan Zoller. These persons enrich the ministry of the whole people of God. Their ministries bridge Church and world. Their ministries are sacramental as they encourage and assist others to claim the call of God and the gifts of love, grace, and justice that God so freely offers a hurting world.

CHAPTER ONE

A Deacon's Heart

"A deacon's heart" is how she described it. An ecumenical gathering of twenty persons from four denominations and three orders of deaconesses was meeting. As the discussion shifted to describing how everyone felt about the agenda, Nancy, a professor at a Lutheran theological seminary and director of a program for diaconal ministers, joyously shared, "From the moment I arrived here, I felt like we were a community. We share convictions and commitments. This happens every time I gather with deacons, deaconesses, and diaconal ministers. We share a 'deacon's heart.' "

"A deacon's heart." What is that? As Nancy further explained, deacons share a commitment to service, to the healing of the creation, to the shared ministry of clergy and laity, and to supporting one another on the journey of faithfulness. For more than a century, deaconesses have embodied ministries of healing and teaching in churches, settlement houses, and hospitals. Since the 1960s, several denominations of Christian churches have embraced the importance of servant ministries and renewed the Order of Deacon. Deacons, deaconesses, and diaconal ministers have joined together in lifelong service ministries of justice and hope.

Vatican II, held during the 1960s, was a renewing

conference for Roman Catholics that reemphasized worship life, clarified that ministry is the responsibility of all Christians, and renewed ministries of healing and justice for God's earth. These shifts gave new life to the Roman Catholic order of deacon as the Church sought ways to implement its ministries of service. Joining this renewal have been Lutheran churches around the world, Episcopal churches, The United Church of Canada, The British Methodist Church, The Methodist Church of the Caribbean, and United Methodists.

In 1976 the United Methodists approved the lay office of diaconal minister and in 1996 the new order of clergy deacon was approved. "The deacon embodies the interrelationship between worship in the gathered community and service to God in the world" (*1996 Book of Discipline* [hereafter known as *BOD*] par. 310). The new order works alongside the ordained elder, whose responsibilities are to lead congregations and to empower persons in the congregation to go into the world as disciples. The new ordained deacon is to lead the baptized people of God in discipleship so that they might be servants of God's saving grace and transformation in the world.

The United Methodist legislation grounded the ministry of the deacon in the earliest church. "From the earliest days of the church, deacons were called and set apart for the ministry of love, justice, and service; of connecting the church with the most needy, neglected, and marginalized among the children of God" (*BOD* par. 319). A deacon's heart is embodied in those ministries of service and justice that connect the Church with the world, with the needy, neglected, and marginalized—ministries that connect the work of the people of God in everyday life with the sacramental, teaching, caring, and saving ministries of the churches. Deacons, laypersons, or elders can engage in these ministries; yet the unique task of the deacon is to be the one responsible for seeing that the tasks of bridging world and work *are* done.

"A deacon's heart," Nancy named it well. Look at what she listed:

- Service: bridging word and world
- Healing creation: the goal of the bridging
- Encouraging shared ministry: building mutuality
- Supporting each other: creating an Order of Deacons to provide care and encouragement and creating structures that connect spiritual formation, service, and life.

From the literature about the deacon, it appears that a deacon's heart is a conjunctive term, meaning "and" or "with." It connects and bridges the mission of the Church with the lives of the people of God. In fact, several theological seminaries report that the presence of deacons training alongside elders has intensified the conversations about the ministry of the laity or people of God. Connections between faith and all life are enhanced.

The elder is involved in full-time "servant ministry" leading in congregations. Elders build up congregations as transforming centers of empowerment and ministry that change lives, call persons into discipleship, and affect the way we live. The people of God (laity) live these ministries in the world. Yet while the people of God may embody in their work a ministering attitude and a serving and witnessing presence, laity are not accountable to The United Methodist Church in the way that ordained persons are.

The representative and leadership nature of the work of those whom the Church has ordained means that the Church must scrutinize all they do. Deacons and deaconesses serve as authorized "servant leaders" modeling and equipping laity for ministries of love and justice such as nursing care, social work, community organization, and Christian education. Deacons are agents of service and change. They bridge Word and worship, Church and world. They serve as path breakers, marking the way for

17

the people of God whose everyday lives are transformed when they live in service to God. They enhance the partnership of all of the people of God in ministry.

In fact, the action of the General Conference of The United Methodist Church in 1996 may be one of the most significant moments in the history of the Methodist churches. Across the United States and around the world, people are discovering that those who are focusing on the healing of creation in ministries of service, justice, compassion, and reconciliation are also in *representative* servant ministries of the Church in that they re-present the love of Christ. This is a revolution in the practices and meanings of ministry.

Margaret Ann is the Director of MA Programs and Deacon Studies at Garrett-Evangelical Theological Seminary. She gets many calls about ministry and specialized ministries. Some are from laity who want to know how to be better laity. Sunday school teachers call wondering if they might take a course about the New Testament. Some who call want to become pastors. Others call because someone has said, "You are describing the ministry of a deacon." They say to Margaret Ann, "I don't know much about being a deacon. What is it? How do I become one?"

For instance, a laywoman called recently. She said, "I've visited in a juvenile detention center with a group from my congregation. I'm at a time in my life when I can commit full time to prison ministry. I hear the gospel call to this work, but where do I get my training? Will my church support this work? Do I continue to develop my skills and calling as a layperson? Or is God calling me to ordained leadership?"

Or another says, "I've served effectively as an administrator in a corporation. I worked as a human relations director. I want to spend the rest of my life helping people claim the gifts God has given them as human beings and learn how they can be used in service of God."

Both of these persons have felt the call to full-time Christian service of love and justice, of empowerment and faithfulness. These persons are not preparing for exclusively congregational ministries. Their ministry complements and expresses the work of the Church. They expand the horizons of ministry in everyday life and equip laity for the work.

The 1996 General Conference affirmed the call of persons to explore ministries that connect Word and world, worship and service. Statements have been written on what the Order of Deacons means. In this book, we build on those statements by focusing on the stories of the people who are actually serving as deacons. Through survey and conversations, we have explored with deacons their commitments and how they are living their ministries in the world.[1] We have asked them what ordination means and how they define the ministry of the deacon. Our hope is to describe the deacon both in terms of the theological definitions that are given to it by the ecumenical Church community and also through the actual ways people seek to be theological and to practice ministry as United Methodist deacons.

The deacon in full connection broadens the definition of authorized ministries of servant leadership in ways that are yet to be fully realized. As The United Methodist Church and the wider ecumenical Church seeks to live into this new possibility, we hope this volume will witness to the voices of those who are deacons, of those who experience, define, and embody the meaning of ordained service in their everyday lives. These voices come from persons who have heard God's call to ministries of service and have answered, "Here am I. Send me." We believe that these voices will enlarge the possibilities for and enrich the dialogue about ministry in our world.

"A deacon's heart" is a heart for all ministries, a heart that sees the abundance of need in our world and the brokenness of creation. This heart calls all of us to transforming ministries of service, compassion, care, education, witness, and justice. The Church needs persons who seek to embody baptismal vows in families and workplaces. We need persons who make a lifetime commitment to congregational leadership. We need persons who dedicate themselves to living the ministries that seek to heal God's creation. A deacon's heart is not the exclusive possession of an ordained deacon for it is the impetus of all ministry and care, the impetus of *diakonia* (service). Yet, the ordained deacon is one who seeks to embody and model this heart for the rest of ministry. The deacon serves the needs of the world, encourages others to serve, and creates settings that equip and empower service. For the ordained deacon in full connection, the call for the healing of the world, the vocation of transforming ministries, and daily work become one.

Join us on this exploration of those who call themselves deacons. Enter into the abundance of need in the world. See what the images of incarnation, of bridge, of empowerment, of community, and of sacrament mean for those who call themselves deacon. See how the deacon is conjunctive, bridging the Word and world. The "and" of the deacon helps those who define themselves as ordained elders to claim the ministries of congregational leadership. The "and" of the deacon also helps laity extend the vocation of baptism into all of life. The deacon can be a sign of a new partnership in ministry.

The group nodded as Nancy thanked them and acknowledged the "deacon's heart." The group knew what she was saying, but they also knew that Christian faith is really about the transforming grace and love of a God who works to heal the brokenness that threatens creation. *Diakonia* is a sacrament of renewal and hope as it proclaims and witnesses to the love and grace of God. *Diakonia* also offers education and empowerment, so that the creation that is "still groaning and is in pain" might be "set free from decay and would share in the glorious freedom of [God's] children" (Romans 8:21, 22 CEV), set free to build new structures of human community, set free to forgive and live in community and justice, set free to unite all people in the love of God, and set free to empower the healing of the world broken by selfishness and sin.

God's grace empowers leaders for full-time ministries of congregational life and care. The hope of God's grace strengthens us as we risk living into the possibilities waiting to be borne by God's children. The deacon's heart brings to life the reconciling love of Christ in ministries that bridge worship and work.

CHAPTER TWO

An Abundance of Need

Deacons in Ministry and Service

In Mozambique, a United Methodist deacon holds a child whose leg and eye were lost in the blast of a long-hidden land mine, comforting, healing, and loving in the name of Jesus Christ and The United Methodist Church. Mozambique struggles to climb out from the oppression of colonialism and the destruction of civil war. Land mines still lurk in the soil, ready to kill or maim. Children, playing innocently in the dirt, can detonate them. In the northern part of Mozambique, this horror plays out over and over. The United Methodist Church of Mozambique, in its effort to respond, has established a home for children maimed by land mines. Bishop Joao Machado proudly claims this vital ministry as the work of a United Methodist deacon, embodying the love of Christ as she seeks to heal the broken bodies and wounded spirits of these innocent children.[1] This deacon is a healer.

Bishop Machado talks passionately about how people in the northern parts of her country, who have been displaced by war, are taught by another deacon how to keep water supplies safe and provide healthy diets for children.

This deacon works with families to teach ways of improving water quality and health. She gathers young mothers and shows them how to care for their children so that they will be protected from the diseases that have come in the wake of a civil war and subsequent upheaval. She advocates for education and brings the compassionate love of Christ to all she meets. This deacon is a teacher as well as a healer. Both deacons are enhancing the lives of people living in difficult situations.

In churches across the United States, deacons—gifted and called to the teaching ministries of the Church—lead the people of God in the servant ministry of Christian education. For instance, deacons plan Vacation Bible School (VBS) with the help of lay volunteers. Children come to meaningfully decorated classrooms, learn songs about God's love, and live into the ancient stories of their faith. Teachers, volunteering their time for this intensive week, are prepared with curriculum and a teaching plan. The week of VBS helps everyone involved—children and adults—to grow in faith and understanding of what it means to be a disciple of Jesus Christ. Many deacons are employed in congregations where they help to organize the life of the congregation for making disciples. Educators lead laity as they create contexts for learning for all ages, contexts where the Word is shared, interpreted, and acted upon. One deacon describes her work: "I see my ministry as a way of helping people grow in their personal lives, grow in their faith, and respond to their own calls to serve."

A lawyer whose specialty is working in children and family services—abused and neglected children, children whose parents fight for custody—now does her work as a deacon in The United Methodist Church. Her ministry is to embody God's love with the social workers and other staff who become so worn down by the suffering they see in the eyes of the children with whom they work. Job tasks have not changed much, but now she focuses on

23

helping the workers clarify their vocations as persons of care, justice, and faith. She builds networks of support and care for these workers.

Another deacon, whose ministry is in administration at a United Methodist seminary, says, "My position is my job, because it pays my bills and provides benefits. It is also my ministry because of the way I encounter my job and the way I do my job." She sees each new student who seeks academic preparation for ministry as an opportunity for service that offers Christ. Her work in preparing classrooms, keeping records, securing professors, and arranging educational contexts is equipping the people of God for service in the world, the work of a deacon.

Another deacon serves her Annual Conference as a mediator for churches in the midst of conflict. She has trained for this ministry and brings the healing and reconciliation of God to hostile and hurting congregations. She calls it a "Pentecost" ministry, "whereby I help people to understand one another with their common bond of Christianity at the core. I do this through conflict resolution, team building, and leadership development." She moves from place to place in her Annual Conference, bringing the Pentecost gift of understanding across differences as she goes. Congregations that have been torn apart by discord find new life through her work of reconciliation; brokenness is healed. Laity who could not communicate with one another are brought into relationships that enable listening and healing.

A social worker is completing her theological degree and hopes to be ordained to the ministry of service and justice, which is her work in a public school in the Chicago area. She has been a social worker in this elementary school for several years, but always felt that something was missing. When she learned of the ministry of the deacon, her call was fulfilled. Her congregation is supportive as she enthusiastically prepares for ordination. The elementary school was at first a bit anxious about the possibility that she might make the school a site for religious recruitment, yet they know the care and respect with which she engages in service. It is clear that some of the teachers need to talk about vocation and some of the families need resources that can only be found with the mutual cooperation of school, church, and family. Her ministry makes these links.

A music minister lives out his call from God helping persons to experience God's presence as they make music together for a worshiping congregation of United Methodists. He speaks of the music as "offering another utterance beyond speech," which proclaims the Word. He says we "offer our best to God and God's people." He speaks with joy of trying to find new ways each week to touch hearts and minds through music that complements the biblical text for the worship service. "I came to this church bringing ministry as what I do. Music is the tool of my ministry." His ministry of proclamation through music reaches out across the age spectrum. "We have eleven choirs here," he says proudly. "We start children at age two." Simple songs such as "Jesus Loves the Little Children" orient the youngest children to the issues of justice that motivate the lives of Christians. Rhymes and tunes are powerful memory aids. Often the scripture passages we remember best are those we know through song. These ministries of music are teaching the Word and calling the people of God to embody that Word in their lives. The Word etched in memory through song is a powerful former of values and actions.

Another music minister sees her work as beginning with proclamation of God's Word. "If we understand the texts that we sing, then it makes an impact on how we respond in the workaday world." Her music connects worship and the world. For her, proclamation through music is particularly effective because of the affective quality of musical expression. "Music changes hearts," she says. She spoke of a man in her choir who employs immigrants in his business. He testifies to the connection between the Word of God he experiences in the music and his commitments to becoming a more just employer. "I struggle personally with how I'm impacting the world," she says. "Making beautiful music can become an end in itself. But I seek to empower and equip everyone in my choir and those who hear us in worship to be faithful to the gospel in all aspects of their lives. I celebrate with those who find ways to bring the love of Christ to the world."

Still another deacon is appointed to a small publishing operation where she edits, writes, and distributes devotional aids to the sick and grieving. She is clear and passionate when she speaks of this ministry. She resonates with C. S. Lewis's image of the Christian faith being like scissors: one blade represents spiritual life and one social action. Neither can work without the other. In addition to this publishing ministry, she also travels to tell the mission story of the United Methodist work she has seen in Congo and Chile. She has struggled to make sense of this dual calling that has no obvious name or focus. It is awkward, she says, when it comes to filling out forms. " 'What is your ministry?' Well, it takes a paragraph to explain." Yet, it is work for which she is called and gifted. She is engaged in telling the gospel story in both settings, keeping both blades of the scissors in use. "I am convinced," she says, "that if we are to see the full fruits of the 1996 General Conference with regard to the deacon, we need to encourage and nurture so many new forms of ministry that we can't possibly name them all!"

A student in the seminary is gifted as a writer and convinced that he must work for justice. After college he spent a one-year internship with *Sojourners* magazine and envisions a ministry some day as an ordained deacon using the skills and power of journalism to work for justice. He is aware that his privilege as a White male creates power dynamics wherever he goes. But he is also willing to use his language and communication skills to aid those who may be less powerful or whose voices are not heard. He is preparing for this ministry with excitement and the heart of a deacon.

The office of deaconess, which we described earlier, actually is a predecessor to that of the deacon in The United Methodist Church. Their ministry of *diakonia* set the model for the ministry of the new deacon in many ways. For instance, at a United Methodist home and school in a pocket of poverty in the mountains, a deaconess embodies God's love as she serves as a principal. Her work is explicitly theological as she helps other teachers reflect on their vocations through teaching. Because it is a United Methodist school, they teach the faith in classes, make connections between their work and the ministries of the Church, and hold up the ideals of ministry and service to the youth with whom they work. They also extend care, education, and physical support to families in the area—families who seek a better life.

Another deaconess serves as a nurse in a United Methodist clinic and hospital in Africa. Her work combines the ministries of healing and care with health education and advocacy, all with an explicit theological statement of the hospital's embodiment of Christ's life of proclamation, care, and healing.

Another predecessor office was the diaconal minister. These persons remained laity but were theologically trained and accountable to The United Methodist Church. They served in ministries of love, service, and justice. They worked as musicians, business managers, administrators, and Christian educators, to name a few of the key vocations.

The deacon in full connection, ordained to ministries of Word and Service, requires a full commitment on the part of both the Church and the deacon. The deacon and the whole Church have the greatest accountability to one another of any of these forms of *diakonia*.

Each person whose story we tell and whose understandings we share in this book is a human being, faulted and loving. Each is also called by the God in whom we have hope. God empowers their ministries of service and their encouragement of the service of others that proclaim the gospel to a wounded world. A wide variety of ministries of justice, compassion, and reconciliation builds bridges between Church and the needs of the world. Soul-filled human beings respond to God's call and God's empowerment in unique ways as they claim the ministry of the ordained United Methodist deacon.

The United Methodist Deacon

What do these people with widely differing skills and places of employment have in common? All are deacons in The United Methodist Church. Each begins with a desire to respond to a need in the world and a sense that his or her gifts are appropriate to meet that need. Each shares a deacon's heart. Each is called by God, prepared for ministry through academic study and a candidacy process of discernment, and ordained by the Church for a lifetime ministry of Word and Service. Note this flow, for it is crucial to understanding the ministry of the deacon. God calls deacons through the needs of the world for healing, justice, and transformation. Deacons are shaped and tested by the Church in the spiritually formative processes of candidacy. Deacons are prepared academically through both graduate theological education and education in the tasks of service, such as education, social work, journalism, nursing, law, public health, or creative arts.

Each sees her or his ministry as encouraging the linking of worship in the gathered community with service to God in the world. Deacons serve in specialized ministries in a wide variety of settings, some primarily in the world and others within the structures of the Church. Therefore, the links occur in a myriad of ways.

The explicit linking of worship and work or Word and Service, however, is the distinctive ministry of the deacon. The ministry of the deacon is found not only in The United Methodist Church. We can learn about the ministry of the deacon from our ecumenical sisters and brothers. As a video about Roman Catholic deacons communicates, deacons are a "living sign to the servanthood of the church."[2] The work deacons do is a sign of the love of Christ. The person of the deacon is a sign everywhere he or she goes of the ministry of the Church. "Deacons bring to the world in which they work and live the values and the message of Jesus in a very tangible way."[3] By embodying their calling in the world, deacons bring the Church to the world, often in places where the Church has not been present.

When the Church examines a deacon's life and witness and certifies that work as an ordainable vocation, the deacon becomes an extension of the Church. The deacon's ministry is "a primary representation of God's love" in the world (*BOD* par. 303.2). The life of the deacon calls the church to faithfulness—pointing to the wounds of creation that cry out for healing. The life of the deacon also empowers faithfulness as the deacon calls and prepares persons through the Church, as agents of God's love, justice, and charity in the world.

The life of the deacon focuses the ministries of all God's people. Through a lifetime vocation and work, the deacon is a model, a sign, that names and empowers the ministries to which we all are called. Faithfulness is lived out as an agent of God's love, active in everyday life, in the midst of a hurting world. Our volunteer service in the church's ministries of nurture or of support and care are faithful embodiments of God's grace. In addition, the daily efforts of all baptized Christians to be faithful, to extend our lives to care for others, and to seek to build justice and loving communities are tangible embodiments of God's grace. The ministry of the deacon leads, teaches, empowers, and focuses these efforts at faithfulness on the part of all.

The Healing of Creation

Come, we that love the Lord, and let our joys be known. . . .
We're marching to Zion . . . the beautiful city of God.
—Isaac Watts, "Marching to Zion"[4]

What holds all of the ministries of *diakonia* together is a common goal of working, with God, toward the healing of creation. Overcoming the forces that separate humans from God and from one another, overcoming the forces of injustice and oppression, and overcoming the wounds that threaten the Body of Christ, is the calling of all Christians. God calls, and some persons respond to the call to ordained ministry because they want to lead and participate in these ministries of healing and compassion, or, as the Roman Catholic deacon expresses it, "Deacons are ministers of justice and charity."[5] Deacons lead other faithful persons marching to Zion.

We all know the extent and depth of the need. We live in a broken world, a world broken by hatred and ethnic cleansing, where wealth divides and buys privilege, where access to the resources of health, hope, and community are rationed, and where the creation itself groans under the pressure of the destruction of air, water, renewable resources, and creatures.

There is an abundance of need. God calls all to march to Zion to create a new heaven and a new earth where there are no tears and justice is everywhere; to work to transform souls and turn them around to be open to neighbor, community, and love; and to transform the very structures by which the world is built.

Yet, in The United Methodist Church, as in most

Protestant mainline churches, we tend to act as if an ordained minister is a pastor, a shepherd of the flock, a professional who presides at marriages and funerals, baptisms and the Holy Eucharist. Moreover, the description of the ministry of the elder is usually Word (study, teaching, interpretation, and preaching), sacrament (the official rituals of the Church that are means of grace), order (overseeing and empowering the work and ministries of a congregation), and service (engaging in ministries in the world). These tasks are all critical for the upbuilding of the Church and the empowering of persons for ministry.

Historically, the tasks of the pastor have been greater. Early in the development of the United States, in the eighteenth and much of the nineteenth centuries, many of those persons serving as pastors were seen as the *parson* of a community, that is, the key person in the community who called the church to extend service, the ministry of Christ, into the world. The parson educated people in faith and life in the name of God; marked key moments of life such as birth, marriage, and death with sacraments in the name of God; and built up the community of faith and its witness in the world in the name of God—that is, the parson ordered the church for witness and service. In these ways, the parson engaged in service in all the moments and aspects of life. The tasks described above that were all a part of the role of parsons may today be shared among elders, deacons, and laity.

Our United Methodist commitment to the ministry of all the baptized reminds us that our ordained leaders are not substitutes for the ministries of all of the people of God. In fact, baptism is the primary ordination for service in the name of Christ. As we are incorporated into the Body of Christ through baptism, all Christians are part of the efforts to bring the love of Christ to the world. The organic image "Body of Christ" teaches us that no portion of the effort is expendable. All parts, though varied and highly differentiated, are essential to the life and work of the Body.

31

The people of God are themselves servants of the gospel, witnessing, loving, and caring in the midst of life. Too often in the contemporary world, with a professional definition of work, pastors become substitutes for the ministries of all disciples. The ordained shepherd has become the professional minister—professionally trained in interpreting the faith, in offering pastoral counseling, and in participating in acts of ministry. Congregations then "hire" professionals to complete the services that they desire. Of course, ministry needs as much competence as possible. That is a gift of professionalism. Yet, professionalism robs call, vocation, and service from the people of God, reserving these for an ordained elite.

The deacon too could become a substitute model of professionalism—a nurse or social worker alone carrying out God's vocation. Again, competence and the division of labors in life are crucial. We must remember that we are not alone in this vocation; God is alive in the midst of the world. God is seeking the healing and renewal of creation. God calls us all as partners in the healing of persons, social systems and communities, and in creation itself. That healing needs all the people of God engaged faithfully in ministry throughout everyday life.

With the coming of the ordained deacon, innumerable visions of the work of the ordained are emerging. The examples beginning this chapter are but a tiny sample of the ministries to which God is calling United Methodists. All Christians are called through baptism to pray and seek God, to study and immerse themselves in interpreting the faith in life, to live lives worthy of the gospel, and to engage in service *(diakonia)*—that is, to be deaconlike. The ministry of the deacon is to embody for the Church the lifetime call and the full-time service of ministry, to be a sign of the ministries to which all Christians are called in their daily lives. Deacons equip the baptized for servanthood.

The 1996 General Conference Action

When the 1996 General Conference of The United Methodist Church adopted a new plan of ministry, it departed from some practices that had been part of Methodist tradition for over two hundred years. Old terms had new meanings for United Methodists. The word *deacon,* which was the term denoting a first ordination of a pastor to a probationary relationship with the Annual Conference, now referred instead to a person in full connection with the Annual Conference who has been ordained to a specialized ministry of service and Word. The General Conference added the commissioned ministry period for a time of probation before ordination for those preparing to be either elders or deacons. The term *deacon* now refers to an order with a new purpose and new relationship to the Church.[6]

The old/new office of ordained deacon in full connection came into being with the 1996 General Conference. However, the Christian Church has designated some of its functions for a deacon since the earliest Christian communities were organized. The specific functions reserved for the deacon and its place in the order of the Church has varied widely. Deacons have served in many capacities through the twenty centuries of Christianity. In The United Methodist Church since 1996, however, *deacon in full connection* has meant a person ordained to "a lifetime ministry of Word and Service." (*1996 BOD* par. 320.1)

> Deacons fulfill servant ministry in the world and lead the Church in relating the gathered life of Christians to their ministries in the world, interrelating worship in the gathered community with service to God in the world. . . . It is the deacons, in both person and function, whose distinctive ministry is to embody, articulate, and lead the whole people of God in its servant ministry. (*1996 BOD* par. 319)

The deacon, as it is currently conceived in The United Methodist Church, remains focused on *diakonia.* The

33

term *servant ministry* was newly emphasized in the *1996 Discipline*. Earlier in the life of the Church, the term *representative ministry* was used to name the distinction between those who were set apart among the whole of baptized Christians by ordination. In 1996 *servant minister* replaced the emphasis on representative. However, the word *representative* has a long and respected place in the history of ecumenical Christianity, denoting the authorization of one's ministry. The word *service* is emphasized to focus on the ministry of all baptized Christians, as well as elders and deacons.

> Within The United Methodist Church, there are those called to servant leadership, lay and ordained. . . . The privilege of servant leadership in the Church is the call to share in the preparation of congregations and the whole Church for the mission of God·in the world. The obligation of servant leadership is the forming of Christian disciples in the covenant community of the congregation. (*2000 BOD* par. 115)

Although the current understanding of the Church is that elders are ordained to Word, Sacrament, Order, and Service, and deacons are ordained to Word and Service, service is the work of all Christians who respond to God's call and claim upon their lives.

The term *elder* or *presbyter* has had a variety of meanings and functions also through the centuries of Christianity. In The United Methodist Church currently, the elder is a full member of the Annual Conference, ordained to a lifetime ministry of service, Word, sacrament and order. "They are authorized to preach and teach the Word of God, to administer the sacraments of baptism and Holy Communion, and to order the life of the Church for mission and ministry" (*2000 BOD* par. 323).

Of course there has been some confusion about these new understandings and practices. Although the deacon in full connection does not itinerate, the traditional mark of clergy in Methodism, the deacon's role relates to an Annual Conference in much the same way as that of other clergy, especially the elder. This adds to the confusion. What is the distinction between elder and deacon when many deacons do things that elders do and many elders do things that deacons do?

Deacons in full connection are helping to define themselves as they seek to serve God. After prayer and discussion, Annual Conferences are continuing to ordain, consecrate, commission, and certify persons for ministries to which God has called them. These persons are seeking to carry the hope of the gospel to a hurting world.

In spite of the ever-present ambiguity and confusion, The United Methodist Church continues attempting to be faithful to its mission to make disciples. Creation groans in its "bondage to decay" (Romans 8:21 RSV). The mission of the Church to bring the "glorious liberty of the children of God" (Romans 8:21 RSV) to fulfillment is incomplete. An abundance of ministry remains to be done.

Redefining Ministry

Following the changes of the 1996 General Conference, the organization of the orders of ordained ministry in The United Methodist Church has become messy and ambiguous. However, out of this chaos and confusion can come vitality and creativity hitherto unknown since the earliest days of the Church. This book will argue that the ordained deacon in permanent connection created by the 1996 General Conference has the potential to redefine the ministry of the laity and reinvigorate and refocus the ministry of the elder.

Leonardo Boff, a Latin American theologian writes of what he calls "ecclesiogenesis."[7] What he means is the rebirth *(genesis)* of the people of God *(ecclesia)*. Boff is writing out of the experiences of the base communities (the most basic and concrete form of small communities of faith) in Latin America where the people of God have begun to meet weekly in study and covenant groups to search the Scriptures and to discern their meaning and ministry for daily life. These people still worship on Sunday and take communion in congregations and cathedrals, but they receive support, care, study, and empowerment in the covenantal base communities. Often a priest or educator meets with the people as an animator or catalyst that seeks to animate faithfulness in people. People encourage one another to share their lives—reflect on them biblically and theologically, support one another through crises and trials, and live as people of God building communities of faith and justice.

The deacon can be an example of how ministry can be animated and extended from the church house, its church schools, and ministries of nurture allowing others to see God's hope emerging in the daily lives of people. We believe that recognizing the diaconal ministries of education, care, legal support, meeting human need, and healing creation as representative and servant ministries will be a sign to the whole people of God that hope and community building are possible and called for by God.

Of course, we realize that the ordination of deacons has the potential to do just the opposite—to devalue the ministry of the laity. Hierarchies could be reinforced where full-time commitments to ministry through the Church are valued over the faithful living of daily life. If the deacon becomes part of a new hierarchy, it will be destructive to the Church and to the purposes of God. Yet, we do not see this hierarchical effect in the people we have interviewed.

We see a transformation of the Church. Little do we know today what this ministry of the deacon has unleashed upon the Church! The hope is that the bridge between Church and world will be enhanced and the ministry of all baptized Christians both reemphasized and resourced. If the ministry of the whole people of God is expanded as new options for service are seen, the ministry of the deacon will have been transforming. If a new partnership can be developed among people who work together in ministry, then the ministry of the deacon will be at the heart of a movement of true *ecclesiogenesis,* of the rebirth of the Church into the servant people of God.

Being a Deacon: God's Call to Transforming Ministry

Let's listen to the voices of deacons involved in this transformation. A deacon, who is a social worker, writes, "It was Jesus Christ's servanthood ministry I wanted to imitate." He understands his calling to be God's "instrument of peace, justice, and love to those who suffer from inhuman treatment and betrayal from their intimate families and communities." His work complements the existing ministries of the Church. "My ministry as deacon aims at filling the gap of the existing ministry of our institutionalized Church and the unmet needs of God's children in secular communities." His identity as a deacon is found in responding to God's call to serve alienated and wounded human beings. "By constantly challenging the tyrant elements of our Church and society, by bridging the alienated elements of human relationship, and by advocating human dignity and the rights of vulnerable people, I am working toward widening the scope of God's vineyard." Other deacons we interviewed also claim this servant and partnership ministry to which God has called them and for which the Church authorized them.

A survey, conducted by Susan Wilhauck, of deacons who made the transition from diaconal ministry to the Order of Deacons, revealed a similar attitude. When asked, "What do you see as the joys of being a deacon?" more than half replied "fulfilling my call to servant ministry" and over 40 percent replied, "using my gifts and graces in ministry" and "serving the church to *bridge the gap* with the world (italics added)."[8] Men and women are seeking ordination because God has called them to a mission and they want to be in relationship with The United Methodist Church as they fulfill that calling. They are filling the gap between the existing ministries of the Church and the unmet needs of God's children. They are extending the meaning of ministry. They are signs of the full call of God to *diakonia*.

Calling and identity are the primary motivators for most deacons. A deacon who has served in the role of an urban minister, a Christian educator, and a teacher wrote, "My decision for ordination was primarily about the Church catching up to my call. . . . The Church was making room, giving authority to my call from God. With the ritual (ordination), the community became clearer about my talents and gifts and the authority of my voice in the community."

"Catching up to my call" is a powerful phrase. This woman *knew* God called her to *diakonia*. But the ministry she speaks of is no individualistic call. The community has affirmed that her life, her call, and her work are a servant ministry in the name of the Church.

The deacon is known by his or her identity. Most deacons begin with who they are when they attempt to explain their order. One writes, "I am a registered nurse, so ministry and work are not really separated."

Another says, "Who am I? I am a teacher/educator. I have always been fascinated with the process of learning, both my own learning and that of others, all my life. I have a deep spiritual yearning to know God and to walk with others who yearn to know God. I am a United Methodist. All the pieces of my life seem to come together in a coherent whole in the ministry of the ordained deacon."

A deacon's identity is linked to a commitment to service or *diakonia* and with the Church's recognition of that service. This deacon's fascination with learning is focused on providing meaningful learning contexts for other Christians to explore, discern, and commit to a life of discipleship.

She continues, "Our distinctiveness is re-presenting Christ to the world through our ministry." *It is not what you do, but how and for whom it is done.*

The mandate of the deacon is to link Church and world. A sign of Christ to the world is another way of saying the same thing. A local church educator, who serves as a conflict mediator for her district, explores this metaphor as she explains the mandate of ministry: "Deacons are like road signs. If they are not everywhere, they should be. Because where would we be without road signs? Incredibly lost and hopelessly without direction. Deacons, like road signs, provide direction. They let us know what is up ahead and help us anticipate our arrival. They help us understand what is involved in ministry or how far we will have to go. Deacons identify what resources are available to help us— like gas, food, and lodging. They even identify points of interest along the way. In short, deacons (and road signs) help us connect with a location or vision. We have come to trust road signs just as we can trust deacons to safely provide all that we will need to safely arrive at our opportunity for ministry. The sign's only purpose is to help us. Likewise, deacons are servants whose only prayer is that all Christians everywhere can find their way to fulfillment through ministry in the name of Jesus Christ."

An Abundance of Need

The world is a place of beauty, grace, and joy. However, the creation also groans under a burden of brokenness, woundedness, injustice, and tears. God calls all of us to seek the healing of creation. The Church proclaims God's grace of healing and renewal in the midst of the world.

Yet, the Church is always in need of renewal as well. When the Church isolated itself from the people, orders of monks, friars, and nuns emerged as ministries of education, healing, and service. When monasteries and convents basked in their wealth, God called servants who walked the highways preaching and caring for the lost. When circuit riding pastors settled in communities and led in defining the status of the establishment, women and men of grace started Sunday schools in their homes, held the hands of the needy, and provided light, food, education, and healing to empower people to work for justice.

In every age, God raises up persons who seek to be servants of care and justice. In the last century, the needs of the urban poor and factory workers were so plain. Too many churches settled in sections of towns occupied by the emerging comfortable classes. Ministry too often was defined as the possession of the pastor and women were excluded from leadership. In response, deaconesses became God's missionaries, Sunday school teachers, settlement house directors, and healers of body and soul to care for the lost and the needy.

Today God can use the deacon as a partner to pastors and laity who carry love and care into a hurting world. The stories we have uncovered about deacons are stories of people who seek to work together with others for the healing of creation and the renewal of the Church. The deacons we have interviewed hope that the Church will push out its boundaries and work harder to empower ministries of justice, love, and care. The congregation is needed as the sanctuary of nurture, education, empowerment, and hope. The world is the setting for God's renewing love. Deacons are partners connecting the witness of the Church with the needs of the world.

CHAPTER THREE

Called to Ministry, Authorized by the Church

The United Methodist deacon, as defined by the 1996 General Conference, is connected with a long tradition in Christianity. The New Testament Church, struggling to organize itself in the aftermath of the death and resurrection of Christ, saw a need for a variety of tasks and ministries.

> Now during those days, when the disciples were increasing in number, the Hellenists complained against the Hebrews because their widows were being neglected in the daily distribution of food. And the twelve called together the whole community of the disciples and said, "It is not right that we should neglect the word of God in order to wait on tables. Therefore, friends, select from among yourselves seven men of good standing, full of the Spirit and of wisdom, whom we may appoint to this task, while we, for our part, will devote ourselves to prayer and to serving the word." (Acts 6:1-4)

Much of the precedent for division of ministry tasks today is contained in this passage. In the earliest years of the Church, there was a need to recognize and utilize varieties of callings and skills. As a result, persons took on diverse roles even though clear orders of ministry had not yet been established. The call for ministries began, significantly, with the needs of the world and with the need to witness to the gifts of reconciliation and community embodied in the ministry of Jesus.

Acts 6 is a description of a conflict that had arisen between two groups within the early Christian movement around the fair distribution of food. The Hellenists claimed that the widows among their community were not receiving as much food as the Hebrew widows were receiving. Food was distributed to the widows, those who were most vulnerable and powerless, each day. But some, the Hellenists said, were getting more than others. The argument, thus, was about the fair distribution of goods.

The community did not have the option of deciding whether or not to feed these vulnerable women. Hebrew Scriptures were clear about that:

> You shall not abuse any widow or orphan. If you do abuse them, when they cry out to me, I will surely heed their cry; my wrath will burn, and I will kill you with the sword, and your wives shall become widows and your children orphans. (Exodus 22:22-24)

The fledgling Christian movement, fully grounded in the Hebrew ethic, understood God's mandate to care for widows and orphans. Women were hungry and the food needed to be distributed in a just and compassionate manner.

In response, the community identified certain of its members who were of good character and strong faith. In other words, they sought out those who could model the kind of person God called everyone to be. These leaders became signs for the ways Christians were to interact with one another. They were to be in "good standing" with the community, persons who were respected by all. They were also to be "full of the Spirit and of wisdom." These persons were to be able to discern God's will and act wisely. In short, these persons were to be spiritual leaders. They also needed to be available for this ministry. Perhaps there were people within the movement whose health or family obligations or vocation made them unavailable.

And what were their tasks? "Waiting on tables" was described as a distinctive task, one different from "prayer and serving the word," the priority for the apostles. Yet, waiting on tables was not merely an act of feeding. It was an act of sustaining a community and a practice of the kingdom of God. For us, this image of "waiting on tables," that is, extending the ministry of the eucharistic table, is an image of the ministries of care and thanksgiving from which we draw our theological definition of the deacon and of the ministry of all Christians.

The Eucharist as Model of Ministry

Early in the emerging Christian movement, the Eucharist became

- an act of remembering and participating in the life, love, and actions of Christ, or, in other words, a celebration of union with Christ,
- an act of building up and sustaining the community, the Body of Christ,
- and an act of promise in which the Church and God's glorious future were connected.

At the table, people experienced Christ, built the Body, and hoped for the fulfillment of God's kingdom.

"Waiting on tables" was also filled with and extends all of these meanings. As the realities experienced at the table were extended to those outside, people remembered and participated in the life of Christ, nurtured each other, and found renewed hope in God's kingdom. God's promise of renewing creation was connected with the table fellowship Jesus had had with his disciples and those experiences of table in the resurrection accounts, such as the meals of the community (sharing fish [John 21:12-13]) or in meals of reflection and revelation (the meal on the road to Emmaus [Luke 24:30-31]).

The eucharistic meal became a way of participating in the resurrection of Christ and in the promise of new life offered in God's acts called "kingdom." Hadn't God made a promise to the Jewish people?

> On this mountain the LORD of hosts will make for all peoples
>   a feast of rich food, a feast of well-aged wines,
>   of rich food filled with marrow, of well-aged wines strained clear.
> And he will destroy on this mountain
>   the shroud that is cast over all peoples,
>   the sheet that is spread over all nations;
>   he will swallow up death forever.
> Then the Lord GOD will wipe away the tears from all faces,
>   and the disgrace of his people he will take away from all the earth,
>   for the LORD has spoken.
> It will be said on that day,
>   Lo, this is our God; we have waited for him, so that he might save us. (Isaiah 25:6-9)

The eucharistic meal was filled with God's promise of the Great Banquet.

Through the Eucharist, the people experienced the transformation of the whole creation. As Paul wrote to the congregations in Rome, "I consider that the sufferings of this present time are not worth comparing with the glory about to be revealed to us. For the creation waits with eager longing for the revealing of the children of God" (Romans 8:18-19).

The Great Banquet was both expected and experienced. The promises of God, which were proclaimed and lived by Jesus, were occurring in the lives of the people. They knew what the promise was. God had "been a refuge for the poor, a refuge to the needy in their distress,

a shelter from the rainstorm and a shade from the heat."
God had stilled "the song of the ruthless" (Isaiah 25:4, 5).
This God would conquer everything and give new life.
Again as Paul proclaimed, "For I am convinced that neither death, nor life, nor angels, nor rulers, nor things present,
nor things to come, nor powers, nor height, nor depth,
nor anything else in all creation, will be able to separate
us from the love of God in Christ Jesus our Lord" (Romans
8:38-39). The Eucharist was a proclamation of the reality
of the Banquet of God set by Jesus.

And this Banquet was a reality in the lives of people.
Not only does Luke tell of the origin of the Great Banquet
in the preaching, ministry, and sharing of Jesus, but he
records in Acts the reality of the early community in
Jerusalem:

> All who believed were together and had all things in
> common; they would sell their possessions and goods and
> distribute the proceeds to all, as any had need. Day by
> day, as they spent much time together in the temple, they
> broke bread at home and ate their food with glad and
> generous hearts, praising God and having the goodwill of
> all the people. (Acts 2:44-47)

This community was bound together: participating in the
Resurrected One, serving each other, preaching the good
news of God's gift of salvation. They grounded their lives
in the hope of the promises of the Great Banquet, the
kingdom of God's triumphant feast that renewed all
humans and creation.

Not only is the reality of the eucharistic community
recorded in Acts, but also research on Paul's Letter to the
Romans defines at least two types of eucharistic communities concretely present in Rome.[1] (Note the communities
defined in Romans 16.) In one type of community,
wealthier converts to Christianity (Prisca and Aquila) provided a eucharistic meal for the believers who gathered at
their house. The feast and this sharing were foretastes of

the "feast of rich food, a feast of well-aged wines" promised on the mountain. The people shared their faith together and took portions from the feast to feed the poor and needy.

Moreover, another type of community emerged in the tenements that filled many parts of Rome. Christians lived together. They worked together and lived as neighbors in very cramped quarters sharing their resources and building up the Body of Christ. The households of Rufus, Narcissus, and Urbanus, for example, were real communities where people shared their poverty and their bounty (Romans 16). They "devoted themselves" as Paul described also of Christians in Corinth "to the service of the saints" (1 Corinthians 16:15), which meant caring for the needy, the widow, the orphan, and the stranger.

In this reality of sharing the eucharistic meal—participating in Christ's reality, feeding one another, and living in the hope of the promises of new life and a God who would "wipe away tears," take away disgrace, and defeat death—the differing forms of ministry were born. Paul even proclaimed that the transformed lives of those who were faithful were evidence of the resurrection of Christ (1 Corinthians 15:16-19). The witness and mission of the Church was a very concrete reality in the lives of people in a world divided by class, citizenship, and oppression.

These meanings experienced at the table were also extended into the world in the ministries of *diakonia*. Service ministries were rooted in the vision of the healing of creation. As Paul wrote: "We know that the whole creation has been groaning in labor pains until now; and not only the creation, but we ourselves, who have the first fruits of the Spirit, groan inwardly while we wait for adoption, the redemption of our bodies" (Romans 8:22-23). The healing of creation, a physical or embodied act in the name of the God encountered in Jesus, was the context for the birth of the ministries of service.

As we examine the narrative in Acts, we see that a division of labor among those called to serve on behalf of the community helped the group to function smoothly. Some were called to the study of the word of God. Others were called to the *diakonia,* or service ministries. The vision of tasks of ministry in the early Church is born in the healing of creation, the signs that fulfill the promises of God's Great Banquet where tears are quieted and food is shared and life is renewed.

These persons, once chosen, stood "before the apostles, who prayed and laid their hands on them" (Acts 6:6). The gathered community offered prayer on behalf of these people. In turn, the chosen ones offered themselves, their gifts, and their energies, to the tasks assigned them. In the ritual, the community recognized these persons as those called to specific work and the individuals accepted that responsibility. With God's help, these chosen leaders and the community would seek the healing of creation.

Similarly, today the congregation in which those potentially called into ministry reside must first recognize and recommend them to serve The United Methodist Church as deacons and elders. The community of faith in the wider Church eventually confirms the recommendation along with requiring academic and spiritual preparation, perhaps parallel to the wisdom and spiritual depth that the early Church sought for its leaders and witnesses. When all is in order, those chosen by the Church for a ministry of servanthood (of embodying the Great Banquet) are authorized by prayer and the laying on of hands.

Deacons Extending the Table into the World

Diedra Kriewald argues that the early Christians organized themselves and their leadership as the Body of Christ, the powerful image of church found in

1 Corinthians 12. "Now there are varieties of gifts, but the same Spirit; and there are varieties of services, but the same Lord; and there are varieties of activities, but it is the same God who activates all of them in everyone" (1 Corinthians 12:4-6). The image of a body that values all of its very different parts is powerful. All parts are crucial and must work together for the body to be healthy and functioning. The tendency to create a hierarchy, which valued one part over another, for example, the ministry of clergy over that of laity, developed later.[2]

In the early Church, people gathered around the table together, people shared their lives, people reached out in service, and people lived the promise. In addition to the threefold pattern of deacons, presbyters, and bishops in the early Church, officers in the apostolic Church included subdeacons, readers, singers, evangelists, doorkeepers, virgins, widows, deaconesses, and acolytes. In an organic understanding of ministry, each partner in the Body was essential for the work of the whole.[3]

Kriewald also argues that the work of the deacon traditionally linked the eucharistic meal with the feeding of the poor. In fact, "the deacon was ordained to insure the just distribution of goods."[4] After assisting at the sacramental table, the deacon took food to the empty tables of the poor. Thus, Kriewald asserts, "All other diaconal functions emerged out of the liturgical leadership of the deacon."[5] It was the deacon who knew the needs of the people, bringing those needs to the community of faith for prayers, and bringing the compassion and justice of Christ to those who were in need. The deacon extended the table.

The actions of deacons and deaconesses in the early Church are the concrete embodiment of the Church's attempts to be faithful to the new vision of reconciliation and care learned from the ministry of Jesus and the experience of redemptive existence in the gatherings of the early Church. The title "deacon" emerges early in the

Christian community. First Timothy states that those who wish to be deacons must be "serious, not double-tongued, not indulging in much wine, not greedy for money; they must hold fast to the mystery of the faith with a clear conscience. And let them first be tested; then, if they prove themselves blameless, let them serve as deacons" (1 Timothy 3:8-10). A deacon clearly must be someone well thought of by the community and gifted with "great boldness in the faith."

The roles of leadership that emerged in the early Church were localized. Different communities organized themselves for the building of the Body of Christ and its service. By the first half of the second century, in the *Didache* and the writings of other Church leaders, descriptions were given for authorized Church workers. The realities of the situation often defined the roles and functions of leadership. The leadership and the sacraments, in fact, "belonged" to the Church, in that the Church defined and supported those who accomplished particular tasks for the Church. The presbyter (priest) usually presided over the sacraments, rites, and practices of the Church. The deacon, in turn, carried the ministries of the table into the world.

As the Eastern and Western streams of Christianity began to mature and separate, differences developed, which had begun with the localized patterns of leadership. The Eastern Church enumerated multiple offices including deaconesses, deacons, and presbyters. A deaconess at that time was a matron, usually a widow or a virgin who had means to support herself and others. She was ordained by the laying on of hands, but considered laity. These women were not ascetic. Their ministry was in cities as they fulfilled traditional women's roles such as caring for young widows, children, or the dying and assisting at the baptism of women. The work of the deaconess extended the celebration of the table. The deacon in the Eastern Church was a caretaker for the Church. He was differentiated from a presbyter because he did not preside at the table. Deacons often were those who prayed in worship and brought the needs of the community to the whole body of the church.

In the West, similar offices and tasks were present, the presbyter (priest) and bishop however were more like the "rulers" of the Church, responsible for both the sacramental life of the Church and its organization. Deacons and deaconesses, in turn, extended and carried the ministry of the Church through prayer, love, and service.

Thus, the office of deacon has had many forms and functions. Primary among them were the tasks of taking care of the Church and of extending the ministries of the Church into the world. Running orphanages, sharing alms with widows, and caring for the sick, that is, extending the ministries of the "table" were functions often assigned to the deacon.

Called to Ministry

In the last chapter, we focused on the abundance of need, which has resulted in the wide varieties of ministries in which deacons serve. Connecting the abundance of need with the leading of the Spirit in people's lives results in a call. People are feeling this tugging all over the Church. They see a need in the world and they believe that God is calling them to meet this need.

In Acts 6, the gospel writer begins with the needs of the world. The Hellenists and the Hebrews are in conflict. Apparently the two cultural groups are threatening the unity of the Church. Perhaps the groups spoke different languages and came from different traditions. The term *Hebrews* may refer to Christian Jews who spoke Aramaic, while the term *Hellenists* may refer to Greek-speaking Jews from other parts of the world who also believed in the risen Christ. Many social and cultural differences could have caused tension between these two groups, but this particular conflict seems to have focused on the distribution of food. Widows were hungry; the most vulnerable in the society needed care. Some persons were identified with special gifts for meeting this need and they were authorized by the laying on of hands. These persons led the people of God in ministries of compassion and justice. The needs of the people of God were the starting place for the call.

The call from God is the place where a deacon's ministry begins. Interviews of candidates for ordination by United Methodist Boards of Ordained Ministry and conversations with seminary students in our classes have reiterated the importance of a sense of "call" for those seeking to enter the ministry.

One woman called the seminary seeking information about the courses she would need for ordination as a deacon. "This call is all a big surprise to me!" she said. She has come to see that her work as a physical therapist and as a *doula* (one who assists a woman in childbirth, particularly single mothers) is ministry. In assisting women in childbirth, a doctor or a midwife or both are present for the delivery; the *doula* stands by the woman providing emotional and spiritual support and caring for the woman as she returns home and seeks to find ways to nurture and nourish her new child. "My work as a *doula* is to be completely present for a woman while she is going through labor and delivery. I accompany her through childbirth, standing by her, encouraging her, wiping her brow, assisting with breathing," she said, "and providing unconditional love."

God's call on her life and ministry has become very powerful. She has the skills of a physical therapist, she reaches out sharing God's love and care, and she promises a continuing relationship of support, nourishment, and education. Seeking to understand what this might mean, she has talked with her pastor who said, "Everything you say fits the role of a deacon in full connection." The deacon extends concretely the practices of Christian love and ministry in all of life.

Just as reaching out to the needs of women giving birth is responding to a call, the importance of a call has been central in the ministry of deacons and deaconesses, central to those who sought to respond with love, grace, and justice to the needs of the world. For instance, in 1890 the Reverend Doctor Thomas Bowman Stephenson founded a Wesley Deaconess Order in The Wesleyan Methodist Church, a Methodist denomination in England. The deaconesses who joined the order were responding to a call from God to meet needs in the world. Laceye Warner, whose research has brought this ministry to light, quotes a letter from a participant in a mission led by a deaconess-evangelist. "We thank and praise God for Sister's visit, and pray that you may have many such workers. The Church and the world need them."[6] Deaconesses worked primarily in three areas of service: visiting, nursing, and evangelistic endeavors. The Deaconess's ministry "typically blended each category according to the needs of a particular context."[7]

While the denomination was slow to approve the order, these women who were responding to a call from God and the urgent, unmet needs of the world, preached in open air, wherever they could gather a congregation. Their call did not require institutional approval. They believed that God had authorized their ministry. A 1905 issue of *The Methodist Reporter* stated, "When the Spirit of God touches with fire a woman's lips, we dare not bid her be silent."[8] Both their messages of revival and their very being (as women called by God for ministry) challenged the status quo of the Church and culture. They were persistent in their efforts to gain respectability. The Wesleyan Deaconess was called by God and validated by the Holy Spirit. She offered a ministry that connected body and soul, characteristics similar to the new United Methodist Order of Deacons in full connection.

In some denominations, a story of a "call" that includes some seemingly supernatural or mystical experiences is almost required for a person to acquire authority for preaching and ordination. Elaine Lawless, whose research on Pentecostal women preachers is published in *Handmaidens of the Lord,* found that the powerful and dramatic story of call was essential for Pentecostal women to find acceptance in a branch of Christianity that usually excludes women from leadership.[9] But God's call is not limited to people who will preach.

Although the calling from God has always been an essential mark of those set apart by the Church for ministry, the deacon as currently conceived by The United Methodist Church, is more explicitly focused on needs of the world in order to move toward the healing of creation. Some deacons, to be sure, find their gifts best used in the Church, as Christian educators, as musicians, or as administrators. But increasingly, those feeling the hand of God making a claim on their lives are acting out of the conviction that The United Methodist Church needs to be present in ministries of compassion and justice. Over half of those exploring the possibility of becoming an ordained deacon today are being called to ministries that seek to advocate or work for justice. One of our students, a man working as an environmental toxicologist with a state department of health, has a vision of a ministry that will empower persons to make healthy decisions to eliminate or reduce their exposure to contamination. The Holy Spirit is moving in his life to imagine a more just world. His ministry will seek to protect the environment and God's creatures within it. How can the Church be present for this ministry? This man is seeking to discern the answer as he begins theological study, looking freshly at his work as opportunity for ministry.

When we encounter God's expectations for creation and the conflicting brokenness, suffering, and oppression, we are called to seek the healing of creation. This conviction about mission is consistent with the emphases of the Methodist movement. John Wesley organized his lay and clergy leaders for the mission of his day, to spread scriptural holiness throughout the land. When Francis Asbury began to organize the Methodists in the new United States of America, he sent them out to ride circuits, starting new communities of faith at every crossroads and bringing the sacraments to people on the frontier.

The mission of The United Methodist Church today is to "make disciples." Or, as the *2000 Discipline* defines, "Ministry in the Christian church is derived from the ministry of Christ, who calls all persons to receive God's gift of salvation and follow in the way of love and service. The whole church receives and accepts this call, and all Christians participate in this continuing ministry" (par. 301.1).

All Christians are called to this ministry of salvation, love, and service. All are to seek to live this call in the world. Yet, particular people are called to lead the whole people of God "through ministries of Service, Word, Sacrament, and Order" (*2000 BOD* par. 303.2). Elders are the leaders who preach, teach, administer the sacraments, order the Church for mission and service, and administer the discipline of the Church. Deacons lead in service and equip others for ministry (see par. 303.2).

Therefore, any place where people feel called by God to respond to this mission of salvation, love, and service becomes a potential site for the ministry of a deacon. People with many professions—nurses, musicians, physical therapists, counselors, administrators, educators, environmental engineers, retreat center leaders, spiritual directors, lawyers, and social workers—may be led by God to a ministry that contributes to the Church's mission to make disciples. Deacons commit their work to a lifetime ministry that imitates and calls others to imitate the servanthood of Christ.

How the Church ascertains the authenticity of a call to leadership is complex. As paragraph 304 says, "God's call has many manifestations, and the Church cannot structure a single test of authenticity." District and Conference Boards of Ministry are expected to ascertain with candidates through prayer, conversation, and testing the candidate's gifts, the authenticity of the call. As listed in the remainder of paragraph 304, the candidate is to:

a) Have a personal faith in Christ and be committed to Christ as Savior and Lord.

b) Nurture and cultivate spiritual disciplines and patterns of holiness.

c) Acknowledge a call by God to give themselves completely to ordained ministry following Jesus' pattern of love and service.

d) Communicate persuasively the Christian faith in both oral and written form.

e) Make a commitment to lead the whole Church in loving service to humankind.

f) Give evidence of God's gifts for ordained ministry, evidence of God's grace in their lives, and promise of future usefulness in the mission of the Church.

g) Be persons in whom the community can place trust and confidence.

h) Accept that Scripture contains all things necessary for salvation through faith in Jesus Christ; be competent in the disciplines of Scripture, theology, church history, and Church polity; and possess the skills essential to the practice of ordained ministry.

i) Be accountable to The United Methodist Church, accept its *Discipline* and authority, accept the supervision of those appointed to this ministry, and be prepared to live in the covenant of its ordained ministers.

This list requires evidence of the call from God. The evidence is partly in the character and gifts of the person's life. The list does not speak directly to the nature or quality of the call. Some experience God's calling in a dramatic, beyond-the-normal event. Some experience God's call in quiet, gradual awareness. Yet, the presence of a call is essential.

Nurtured and Educated: Response to the Call

The first deacons were identified by the community of faith for certain specialized ministries. They responded to the call by offering themselves as leaders. They were authorized for their ministries of extending the table by the laying on of hands (what has since been called ordination).

> The early church, through the laying on of hands, set apart persons with responsibility to preach, to teach, to administer the sacraments, to nurture, to heal, to gather the community in worship, and to send them forth in witness. The church also set apart other persons to care for the physical needs of others, reflecting the concerns for the people of the world. (*BOD* par. 302)

The Church retains this pattern today. The community of faith has the authority to choose those who will be its leaders. After a process of preparation by the candidate, he or she is examined. Finally, the ordained uphold the standards of education and preparation for ordination. Their vote is necessary for admittance to the order.

Because The United Methodist Church now has two orders of ordained ministry, a person who feels this tugging must discern which order is most appropriate. This discernment takes place in the candidacy process. Four steps of the process are:

1. The Inquiring Candidate—having experienced a call to ordained ministry, the individual contacts a deacon or elder, reads *The Christian as Minister* and participates in the ministry inquiry process with a guide, such as the person's local pastor (see *2000 BOD* par. 306.1).

2. The Exploring Candidate—continuing the discernment with a mentor assigned by the district superintendent and the district committee on ordained ministry, the person applies to the district superin-

tendent for admission to the candidacy studies (which includes a *Candidacy Guidebook* from the General Board of Higher Education and Ministry) (see *2000 BOD* par. 306.2).

3. Having met requirements for membership and education, the person is interviewed by the pastor and committee on pastor or staff-parish relations and recommended by the Charge Conference (see *2000 BOD* par. 306.3).

4. Continuing to meet all requirements (including a psychological assessment report), the person applies to the district committee on ministry to become a certified candidate (see *2000 BOD* par. 306.4).

The *Guidebook* helps the candidate to consider whether or not ordained ministry is appropriate. Gifts and skills, resources, and the promptings of the Holy Spirit are part of the conversation with a mentor. The process is intended to enable the candidate to clarify and solidify her or his calling to ordained ministry.

The candidacy process requires two years of membership in The United Methodist Church with opportunity to serve in a leadership position. The candidate works through this process with the committees and authorities in the Annual Conference in which he or she is a member of a local United Methodist Church.

Working with one's mentor and through the candidacy processes of the Annual Conference is only one aspect of preparing for ordination. In addition, the candidate must meet academic standards, including both theological education and education in the specialized tasks of one's ministry. For instance, a parish nurse must have both theological education in the Scripture, traditions, and practices of the faith as well as education in the practices and skills of nursing. The routes for academic preparation are multiple. While a master's degree from a graduate theological school approved by the University Senate is the benchmark, alternative academic routes are available.[10]

Commissioned and Accountable

At the conclusion of academic preparation and the candidacy process, and with the recommendation of the Conference Board of Ordained Ministry, the individual goes before the clergy session of the Annual Conference. The ordained deacons and elders in full connection vote on the commissioning of the candidates.

Commissioned ministers are then appointed by the bishop and serve for at least three years as probationary members of the Annual Conference.[11] During this probationary period, the Board of Ordained Ministry is responsible for organizing covenant groups that continue the spiritual and professional formation of the candidate.

Commissioned ministers serve in ministries appropriate to their order. Those planning to devote their lives to the ministry of the deacon must serve in ministries of Word and Service. Those planning to devote their lives to the ministry of the elder must be appointed to ministries of service, Word, sacrament, and order. Commissioned ministers are under the appointment of a bishop and are practicing their chosen ministry whether of pastoral leadership, education, parish nursing, a justice ministry working with an ecology agency, or of legal aid as a deacon. During this time, their education continues within the Annual Conference to sharpen and test gifts and graces for ministry. They are examined as to calling, gifts, character, and effectiveness.

Ordained and Authorized

Candidates who have successfully completed the probationary period and are recommended by the district superintendent and the Conference Board of Ordained Ministry are presented to the clergy session of the Annual Conference. Deacons and elders in full connection may vote. With a two-thirds vote of the clergy members, the probationary member may be admitted into full member-ship and approved for ordination.

"From among the baptized, deacons are called by God to a lifetime of servant leadership, authorized by the Church, and ordained by a bishop" (*2000 BOD* par. 319). The *Discipline* tells us that ordination is "a gift from God to the church" (par. 303). In the same sense that baptism acknowledges entrance into the Church and claims God's promise of grace, ordination acknowledges the calling, gifts, and preparation of the deacon and claims the gifts of the Holy Spirit for ministry. All of this comes to us through the grace of God. Through ordination some are set aside with responsibility for certain functions within the ministry of the Church.

In ordination, the community—that is, the Annual Conference—affirms the gifts, evidence of God's grace, and promise of future usefulness of the deacon. In ordination, the deacon also responds to God's call by offering herself or himself to the Annual Conference for a lifetime of lead-ership as an ordained minister. Thus, both the Annual Conference and the ordinand are affirming and committing themselves around these gifts and acts of service.

Ordination, as we will argue in chapter 9, is the for-malization of the Church's earliest process of laying hands on those who were to work on behalf of the Church in the world. The Church has always decided who could preside at the table. The Church quickly began also to authorize others to represent its ministries of witness, nurture, and service in the world. This authorization was done by the formal act of laying on of hands. Through this act the grace of God was called on to undergird and support the person's ministry. Key was the acceptance and public acknowledgment of this person as one to embody, reflect, or re-present the min-istry of Christ both in the Church and in the public world. Ordination is distinguished by these characteris-tics:

- Continuity: It is an act in continuity with actions in the early Church to recognize leaders. Those actions were called apostolic for they represented the act of passing on the tradition.
- Representative: Through the act of laying on hands particular persons are not only recognized as authoritative witnesses of the Church, they are empowered to be the leaders, witnesses, evangelists, healers, and teachers who are recognized and affirmed as representing the Church. The Church chooses to accept their ministry and decides who presides at the table and who extends the table into the world on behalf of the Church.
- Sacramental: The acts the ordained perform are sacramental in the broadest definition of that word. When these acts re-present the vision, care, call, service, and teaching by which Christ is known and through which come reconciliation, healing, and new life, their acts are sacramental.

The ministry of the ordained elder or deacon is a thread in the fabric of work in the world, which is the ministry of all Christians. Each thread in the fabric is important to its strength and beauty. The threads rest on and undergird one another. The ministry of ordained persons is neither more nor less important than the ministry of other Christians; the ministry of ordained persons equips the ministry of laity in the world even as it depends on the ministry of laity in the world. "The people of God, who are the church made visible in the world, must convince the world of the reality of the gospel or leave it unconvinced" (*BOD* par. 107).

The Great Banquet

Early in its beginnings, the community of faith lived in hope of the Great Banquet. As the people of God gathered at table, they encountered the presence of the spirit, of the resurrected Christ, who connected their lives to the servant and proclaiming ministry of Jesus. Through this meal, they built up their community, sharing their resources and reaching out with love, healing, and charity. Moreover, through the meal they remembered and encountered the reality of God's promise of a feast set on a mountain where the needy, the poor, the disgraced, the sorrowful, the outcasts, the victims, and the hungry could find hope and new life—hope that transcended tears, food, wine, and death. Deacons were persons called and authorized, set apart, nurtured, and formed by the community for service. They extended the ministries of the table and the witness to the Resurrection, the reality of new life in community, and the hope of God's continuing grace and love into the world.

As we have seen, this is the renewal that is occurring in the reality of the deacon. Signs of new life and healing are present in the world. The Church is "groaning in labor pains" to live the promise, grace, and healing to which it is called. The people of God are seeking to respond to the spiritual malnourishment of the age with the Eucharist food of love, hope, and endurance.

Hope is embodied in the deacons with whom we have talked. We now will build on their stories to see how the promises of the banquet and of a new community are being lived. Deacons talk about their ministry as an incarnational one. Deacons build bridges and empower people to seek new life and community. Deacons seek to build community among themselves. Deacons partner in ways that call others into mutual ministry and mutual living.

There is great need. God needs many servants—people of God who seek to be faithful in their everyday lives, people called to build the congregation into an empowering faith community—like Aquila, Prisca, Stephen, and Phoebe, called to embody the realities of the banquet in daily lives. God calls through the world. The Church nurtures and trains people. After testing, the Church authorizes some persons to ordained ministries of elder and deacon.

CHAPTER FOUR

An Incarnational Vocation

"When you just stick around in your churches, you miss Jesus." These words, from a deacon who serves as an administrator for a center for women and children in an urban context, point to the incarnational and sacramental nature of the ministry of *diakonia*. We all have the potential to re-present Christ to one another as we interact in settings of Christian love.

All of us, clergy and laity alike, who seek to follow Jesus, are called to be servants or the *diakonia* of Christ. The ministry of all Christians is to be servant, disciple, lover of God and world, and leader in transformative ministries of love and justice, of healing and care in the midst of the world. Servanthood is not a phrase that is restricted to the ordained deacon or elder. Neither is servant leadership a restricted task.

How, then, can deacons understand and live their ministries and vocations as distinct from those of the general ministry of all Christians? And how do these understandings help us to define the interrelationship of deacons, elders, the people of faith, and all the people of God in the world? The next chapters will explore answers to these questions using the understandings and words of those serving as deacons in full connection, those defining in practice the ministries of deacon.

In this chapter, we will focus on the expressions of deacons about their identity in an incarnational vocation. As deacons live and work, they seek to *incarnate* the ministry of Jesus. One deacon summarizes it: "Our distinctiveness is re-presenting Christ to the world through our ministry." Not all deacons use this language of "incarnation," yet over and over again, we heard deacons refer to their actions by images that can only be understood as incarnating or sacramenting. These deacons affirm that laity also seek through their lives to embody the love and ministry of Christ. Deacons seek both to re-present Christ and assist laity to re-present Christ in their lives and ministries.

When we speak of the ministry of the deacon as "incarnational," we mean that the embodied, concrete person of the deacon has the potential to act in ways that are Christlike.

When we speak of the ministry of the deacon as "sacramental," we mean that the deacon and the actions or ministries of the deacon become a window on the Holy by pointing to Christ or mediating the presence of Christ among us. These images are crucial as we rethink a theology of ordination itself. We will explore the deacons' understanding of mediating the presence of Christ and move to discuss the concern of deacons about the sacraments.

A student, preparing himself for ordination as a deacon, lives with his wife on Chicago's South Side. The neighborhood in which they live has fallen on hard times. Downsizing, lack of technological expertise, and other economic factors mean that many in the neighborhood are unemployed or underemployed, either recently or for most of their lives. He has heard God's call to live among these children of God and to bring hope along with support and training to the neighborhood. His face is the face of Christ, a sacrament of the Holy, when he transforms hopelessness into hope through his ministry. In turn, he talks of the encounter with Christ that he experiences as he works among these persons, many of whom have hung onto their faith even as they have lost their possessions. This ministry is an example of incarnation, a sign of Christ, as it begins the slow process of transforming the lives of those who participate.

The late Joseph Cardinal Bernardin of Chicago wrote in a pastoral statement on the permanent order of deacon named "The Call to Service" that "a fundamental aspect of the deacon's ministry is to model and encourage the development of the servant ministry of all the baptized."[1] The word *model* is the key term that we heard in the words of deacons. By modeling or by re-presenting the service of Christ, the deacon inspires others for ministry.

An Embodied Ministry

Paragraph 319 of the *2000 Discipline* expresses this ministry of incarnation and embodiment, "It is the deacons, in both person and function, whose distinctive ministry is to *embody*, articulate, and lead the whole people of God in its servant ministry" (italics added). As the meaning of the word *diakonia* implies, the deacon serves. When we serve, we are standing in the place of Christ, doing the ministry that is his.

An important distinction must be made here. Deacons do not understand themselves as the incarnation that was Christ; rather a deacon is an instrument through which the grace of Christ may flow to the world. In more classical theological terms, a representative act that serves as a window on the Holy is sacramental. Classical theology has argued that Christ is the sacrament of God, a window or incarnation of the Holy. In turn, the Church is the sacrament of Jesus, offering through Jesus a window on

Christ or the Holy. As the deacon practices her or his ministry of compassion and justice, the work of Christ in the world is made manifest, is advanced and incarnated.

A young woman, finishing her Master of Divinity degree, recently announced that after a long struggle she has discerned that God's call on her life is to serve as a deacon rather than an elder. She had a career doing "social-worker-like" things before she came to seminary, but found that God was asking something different from her. Therefore, she came to theological education seeking to address what she saw as a disconnect between the Church that is to be a light to the nations and the darkness of the world. "The church will die if it's separated from the world. We're seeing some of that death right now," she says. Her call from God, she says, will be to be like a "laser." She envisions her ministry as bringing focused streams of light into the darkness. "I am preparing as a pastoral counselor," she says, "and plan on doing something for the communities that surround the church that will bring healing." The ministry of this deacon has the potential to embody the healing love of Christ.

In the following words, a Christian educator articulates how her ministry embodies the ministry of Christ. Her incarnational approach to ministry also seeks to link the gospel expressed in worship with the gospel incarnated in the world. She says, "I embody the link between worship and work as I lead a Christian education program that attempts to create just and hospitable spaces where members of the community of faith may critique, articulate, and commit to bringing faith to their workplace." In addition, she is clear that this commitment to embodiment is something that she communicates and seeks to instill in those with whom she works. "I articulate the link in all my planning, teaching, and writing. I lead in linking as I witness to the call of God in my life. I stand with one foot in the Church and the other foot in the world, providing, I hope, a listening ear. I bring that link to a lifetime ministry as a deacon." In addition, this educator helps each layperson understand and claim his or her ministry of servanthood in relationship to the ministries of Christ.

Through the deacon, the ministry of Christ is made present for the people of the Church and, in turn, through their ministries, Christ is witnessed to and embodied in the world. The Body of Christ thus becomes the concrete embodiment or presence of Christ in the world through the practices of persons of faith. The deacon we quote above is clear about her identity as she uses the word *embody*. In this case, "embody" is used as a synonym for "incarnate" or "to make present." She is also intentional about the power of her ministry to stimulate ministries of incarnation in others.

A deacon who directs a center for women and children in the inner city sees her ministry as providing a context for servanthood for the people of the church. They and she together "incarnate," make present, the love and grace of Christ. "My ministry is giving people an opportunity to serve in a way they couldn't do otherwise." Volunteers from the church come to help serve lunch to women who are on the streets or hungry. The guests are invited to pray before the meal. In the faith of these poor, illustrated through their eloquent grace before the meal, the more affluent volunteers find a witness to God's presence in the world. The volunteers encounter Christ in the faces of those they serve.

The deacon told of a woman, recently widowed and also grieving the loss of her mother, who still faithfully came to serve lunch to the hungry women. "How can you do this?" asked the deacon. The volunteer replied, "It's healing for me. I see their faith and I am borne up in my sorrow." Those serving in the soup kitchen found Christ there. The ministry of this deacon creates the connection; she embodies the link by which God in Christ is present. The ministry is incarnational and sacramental.

This deacon whose ministry provides meals and after-school care to families in need, describes her ministry as a way of giving laity the opportunity to serve in a way they could not do otherwise. The agency she coordinates provides a structure for involvement in servant ministry. "When you just stick around in your churches," she says, "you miss Jesus." Jesus is seen and experienced in the faces of those who serve and volunteer and in the lives of those who are thereby touched by Christ's presence.

"Know Who You Are"

One's incarnational identity and ministry take many forms. A deacon whose ministry of education consists of teaching life skills to Appalachian women who have been trapped in a cycle of poverty and lack of opportunity recounts a conversation in a class that clarified her identity with incarnational ministry: "As we were talking you could see a lot of hurt coming out and a lot of pain. One of the women with whom I'd shared some faith stories when we were on break looked at the class and said, 'Girls, in the midst of all this we just have to remember who we are!' That just struck me. I think that's what my ministry is with this population—helping them to remember who they are and that they are special and that they are somebody and they can do things. They can be self-sufficient. There are so many barriers—from abuse to lack of transportation or childcare or really very low self-esteem—that seem to tell these women that they can't do anything. I think that really sums up what my ministry is: helping them remember who they are."

The young woman learned who she was. "Girls, in the midst of all this we just have to remember who we are!" Through her recognition, others came to see themselves as valued children of God. They remembered who they most fundamentally are.

This deacon's teaching ministry of compassion and

justice brings the kind of liberation and self-worth to these women that Jesus brought to the women he met. From Jesus' approval of the roles of Mary and Martha to the healing of the woman with the hemorrhage to the open dialogue with the woman in Samaria who becomes an evangelist for the gospel, he helped women to remember who they are and to realize their possibilities. This servant ministry carries the compassion and healing of Christ to the world. This deacon is embodying sacramentally the presence of God for the lives and identities of these young women as she brings healing and hope to their lives.

Through the young woman's call to "know who we are," the deacon, in turn, recognized her own identity. She realized that she is a role model. Her identity incarnates that she too is a child of God. The fact that she is a mother who works and whose relationship with her husband is healthy and mutual teaches these young women.

She tells this story, which illustrates the power of her model for the women with whom she works. Learning about the partnership of this deacon and her husband in parenting, a young woman in the life-skills classes was prompted to reflect on her relationship with men. "We had been talking about nontraditional roles for women and this student said, 'Well, you know, I'm interested in mechanical things. My boyfriend is a mechanic and I can fix anything because I help him all the time.' So at the technical college we went to the class for mechanics. She walked right over to a car. The instructor said, 'I'll bet you don't know what that is.' She proceeded to name everything that he asked her. I was impressed with that and she was just really excited about the possibility of going to school there. We started asking questions about the job market for women and the instructor said, 'Well, it might be hard at first but if you are good people are going to be open to the possibility.' She seemed really excited about the possibility until she said, 'You know, the problem is going to be that my boyfriend is not going to like me being in class with all those guys, and then I would have to work around men too. I just don't think he is going to go for that.' It was just amazing to see how deflated her spirit became when she started considering that."

The deacon not only brings the ministries of justice and compassion to her teaching, but also serves as a role model for new possibilities and relationships. Sacraments extend the grace of God; the life of this deacon is sacramental as God's grace is communicated through the model of her life and family. Deacons "know who they are"; their lives transparently are windows on the love and justice of Christ. They point to others who are also sacramental—windows on the Holy.

Carrying Christ's ministries of compassion and justice to the world is the ministry of the deacon as is stimulating others to faithfully live their ministries. The deacons we have interviewed are coming to claim the incarnational nature of their work. A social worker sees his work as incarnating or imitating Christ's call to the Church to bring healing and reconciliation to all people. He says, "My ministry as deacon aims at filling the gap of the existing ministry of our institutionalized Church and the unmet needs of God's children in secular communities." His embodied ministry brings Christ to the world as he works with Asian American families who are in crisis. He "sacraments" the world. Just as a sacrament extends the grace of God, so too the life of this deacon is sacramental as God's grace is communicated through the healing and justice his ministry brings to families in crisis.

An Authorized Ministry

In chapter 2, a deacon described ordination as "the Church catching up to my call." She always knew that her vocation was to teach and lead. Her identity as a child of God embraced both the gift of compassion and a passion for justice. The action of The United Methodist Church in consecrating her as a diaconal minister and then ordaining her as a deacon meant that the community of faith was validating what she already knew was there. Ordination did not *change* her identity or vocation. However, it brought the official recognition of the community of faith to her identity and vocation, *authorizing* its use on behalf of the Church. Her servant ministry, in the sense that it embraces *who* she is, incarnates God's love. Her leadership, the Church authorizing *what* she does, is vocational. Through her ministry, people encounter the grace of God, are called to new life, and claim their identities as children and servants of God.

Another deacon writes that her starting place was her training and gifts as a teacher. She says, "If I had not felt confident in my work in the world, I don't believe I could have answered God's call to use my gifts and graces as a teacher, practiced and honed in the secular world." Through her educational ministry for the church, "faith stories [are] shared and faith experienced and enlarged." Some deacons bring their vocational gifts and skills from an earlier profession to ministry, changing only the content or focus of the work. In this way, deacons represent how the ministries of the people of faith in the world may become moments of incarnating God's love and justice and calling others to faithfulness.

Deacons can be very passionate about the work they do serving Christ in the world. One, clearly angry with some of those who are seeking ordination as a deacon for what she would call the wrong reasons, wrote, "For me, the *office* of deacon doesn't have the meaning. The work I do has the meaning." In other words, the integrity of a life commitment to bring love and justice (Christ's healing and reconciliation) to the world is going to be there whether or not she is ordained or authorized.

Many diaconal ministers who sought to make a transition into the new role of deacon talked of how the ordination would not change who they are or what God has called them to do. Rather ordination *would* change their relationship to The United Methodist Church and, perhaps, how others view their work. In other words, the Church was officially recognizing their ministries to the world.

Sacramental vs. the Sacraments

A deacon's ministry is sacramental. This, however, is a broader definition of "sacrament" than is typically used. A narrower meaning for the term would include only the official rites of the Church. In the case of United Methodism, only Baptism and Holy Communion are sacraments. In the *Discipline* the official sacraments of the Church are reserved for elders. Deacons assist the elders with sacraments (par. 303.2). Deacons also participate in worship. This liturgical role is a means by which daily work and worship are connected. In fact, some congregations have renewed the practice of the early Church where the deacon led the intercessory prayers of the people. The deacon brings the needs of the people and of the world to the community at prayer and worship.[2]

Many deacons we interviewed spoke about the 1996 General Conference's decision that reserved the right of presiding at the official sacraments of the Church for elders (and those appointed to serve churches as local pastors). In practice, the concrete difference between deacons and elders is often defined by who may preside at the sacraments of Baptism and Eucharist. In fact, a fear has been expressed that if deacons are authorized to preside at the sacraments, they will lose their unique bridge roles and become merely "junior elders," replicating the ministries of the elder in churches.

What distinguishes deacons and elders and, in turn, what distinguishes the ordained from the laypeople in the pew and in the world? Deacons "extend the table." Their ministries are an extension of the Church into the world. Some deacons work in the Church in ministries of Christian education, spiritual formation, or musical and worship leadership encouraging the people of God to articulate, claim, and embody their ministries to and in the world. However, many of those presently training for ordination as deacons are preparing to engage in ministries in the world. Their work will address issues of violence, support ministries with children, and work for the healing of creation. Many will serve as social workers, nurses, doctors, journalists, or counselors. In every case, the ministry of the deacon will take the embodied grace of God to people in marginal situations, in outcast places of living, in institutions of care and healing, and in ministries of advocacy and need.

For many deacons, presiding at the sacraments in a congregation is not an issue. However, for some of these ministering in marginal areas in the world, being able to share the sacraments within their ministries of care is important. For example, the sacraments are critical for deacons on the front lines caring for abused and dying children in a hospital chaplaincy, for a broken family in an advocacy ministry, for those defeated by poverty and living on the streets who seek help through a homeless shelter, or for persons facing surgery for a devastating illness. Those whose ministry of chaplaincy is in a hospital, on a school campus, on a battlefield with soldiers, or with refugees separated from family and homeland by military action and aggression might need to bring the healing power of the sacraments to these wounded people. These deacons feel the need to offer the sacraments—the grace of Baptism and Eucharist—to those with whom they work.

Somehow we need to rethink Church legislation. Practically, deacons do not seem to need rights to preside as sacramental leaders within congregations. Here the ministries of deacon and elder complement each other and elders are available to lead, and deacons to assist, in providing the sacraments of Baptism and Eucharist. For example, deacons who have taught, administered educational programs, and assisted youth as they moved to a confession of faith and to baptism (for those who have not participated in this sacrament as children) can assist elders in the administering of baptism. In this way, elders represent the whole Church; deacons stand by as teachers, witnesses, and evangelists of God's gracious love; and laity accept the persons as members of the community of faith. Wherever deacons and elders work in close proximity, deacons can assist elders in the celebration of the sacraments.

Speaking practically, however, in ministries in the world, where deacons are authorized by the Church and not working in a team that includes an elder, deacons need access to the sacraments. In this way, as deacons fulfill ministries of justice and care to which they are appointed, they can offer the visible and historic signs of God's sacramental grace in baptism and Eucharist.

However, practical necessity is not the only reason to rethink Church legislation about the sacraments. Theologically and historically, the sacraments belong to the Church. The Church in council has decided who can preside at the table and offer the water and grace of baptism. In the early Church, local church patterns developed that met the needs of local bodies of Christ. The Church decided how to offer the sacraments and who presided.

In The United Methodist Church, we have sustained this classic pattern of the Church deciding about sacramental leadership through legislation in General Conference. We have decided that elders have regular rights to preside at table and administer baptism. We have decided that local pastors appointed to a church may administer the sacraments where they are appointed (*BOD* par. 340.1). In turn, we have decided that deacons are involved in liturgical leadership and assist elders in the carrying out of the sacraments.

Deacons "extend the table" as they bridge worship and daily work. It is clearly the right of the church to decide how deacons "extend the table" and assist the elder in sacramental leadership.

We can argue: It is correct for the bishop as a leader of the Church to determine with consultation that a particular ministry carried out by a deacon needs rights of sacramental leadership for the good of the Church, and thereby extending the table into the world. If a deacon, in a particular ministry, were given the right to lead the sacraments, that deacon would then be assisting the elder and the whole Church in extending the table into the world. Decisions about sacramental practice reside with the Church, the Body of Christ. What serves the Body of Christ and extends the mystery of God's grace and justice is to be affirmed.

In their ministries, deacons' acts are sacramental and therefore do not usually need the responsibility of leading in the sacraments. Yet, when the ministry of the deacon calls for the leading of the sacraments to serve the Body of Christ and to assist the leadership of the Church, deacons should be empowered with the rights and responsibilities of leadership.

Also it should be noted that with ordination, the deacon has been authorized to conduct weddings and funerals. Deacons who serve in campus ministry, for instance, are finding that many students request that the deacon preside at their weddings. Deacons, who do social work or chaplaincy with the elderly or ill, will receive many requests from families to conduct funerals. These are extensions of the love of Christ to families at these key points in their lives. An appropriate extension of the ministry of a deacon is sometimes the conducting of a wedding or a funeral.

When they serve Christ in ministry authorized by The United Methodist Church, deacons seek to become the hands and feet and heart of Christ in the world. Therein, the deacon embodies the reconciling love of Christ in an incarnational ministry. Incarnational ministry has the potential to transform wounded people into joyous children of God. Incarnational ministry provides role models for Christian living and discipleship. Incarnational ministry can carry healing to communities torn apart and dispirited. Incarnational ministry is a sacramental ministry, mediating the presence of the Holy in the midst of the realities of life. Incarnational ministry sees the face of Christ in both servant and served, convincing the world of the reality of the gospel.

CHAPTER FIVE

The Ministry of the Deacon: Bridging and Empowering

In a regional state university in the Midwest, two deacons serve in campus ministry. They are husband and wife. Both are licensed professional counselors. They have chosen to share one full-time position so that they also have time for their children and each other. This choice of working half-time is "a major witness of our ministry," they proclaim. Their ministry builds bridges between The United Methodist Church and the students. The ministries of the students also bring the Church to the world. They claim, "Worship is the heart of our campus ministry, our Christian community. We connect to the world by the mission trips we do, by our service. We encourage students to worship at First Church and we are present there to bring prayer concerns from the campus and wider world to that congregation."

At the final examination period before Christmas, the campus ministry offers an opportunity for parents and others to purchase a luminary in honor of a student. All the lighted sacks are placed in a row at the entrance to the campus one evening, a beautiful reminder of the

Advent of Christ and of the caring families who recognize that final-exam week is a time of great stress. The student in whose name the luminary is lighted also receives a card carrying the good wishes of the donor. These luminaries link students, parents, and the Church. They are a message of care and support to the entire university community, their warm glow and their number signaling to all who pass by on the busy thoroughfare that Church and world are connected.

One evening a mother called the campus minister/deacon from the airport, anxious that her business trip had distracted her and she had missed the deadline to order a luminary for her daughter, a university student. "Any chance I can still get a luminary for my daughter? I did it last year. She still has the card." The ministry of these deacons is a bridge that carries the sign of the love of Christ from parent to child, from Church to community, from worship to world.

"Bridge" is a powerful image for the United Methodist deacon in full connection. The ministry of the deacon bridges worship and work or Church and world. In the words of the *2000 Discipline,* "The deacon embodies the interrelationship between worship in the gathered community and service to God in the world" (par. 310). This interrelationship is imaged as a bridge.

As we saw earlier, certain leaders in the early Church assisted at the eucharistic table and then carried the bread, along with other goods, and the love of the community to the tables of the poor. The new deacon has been conceived with that in mind. Connecting the Word—as experienced in the presence of the Spirit and the promise of the Great Banquet—with the concrete realities of feeding people in the world is the calling of the deacon.

"Deacons fulfill servant ministry in the world and lead the Church in relating the gathered life of Christians to their ministries in the world . . ." (par. 319). The *Discipline* continues with a rehearsal of the evolution of the ministry of the deacon, from the earliest Christian communities to the more recent deaconess and diaconal minister. "The ministry of the deacon is a faithful response of the mission of the Church meeting the emerging needs of the future" (par. 319).

The concrete experience of deacons fills out these theological and practical conceptions. As deacons respond to the needs of the world and serve in the Church, the possibilities for building bridges between worship in the gathered community and service in the world are expanding and clarifying.

For instance, leading the prayers of the people in worship each week provides an opportunity to bring the needs for compassion and justice to the community of faith and hold them up for God's healing grace. The two deacons in the beginning of this chapter speak of bringing the concerns of the campus to the congregation in which they worship. When they lead the congregational prayers on Sunday morning, they include the realities of campus life, praying for students and faculty. They ask God's presence for new freshmen students suffering with homesickness. They seek guidance for students who struggle to find vocation. They pray for wisdom in the decisions of administrators who must deal with student discipline.

Deacons such as these, whose ministry spans Church and world, are uniquely situated to lead these prayers. The campus ministers are doing what the *Discipline* refers to as "leading the congregation in interpreting the needs, concerns, and hopes of the world" (par. 319). This reality was a practice in the early Church as the deacon led prayers of petition and intercession—prayers of the people in the eucharistic celebration.

Acting as a Bridge

How does the bridge work? Consider this description from a deacon whose work is in the area of Christian education and conflict mediation: "I saw in the deacon a new and powerful way to uphold and empower laity. Most elders lead congregations. Diaconal ministers work within a congregation or at a specific job in the community. Suddenly the new Order of Deacons offered a very clear mandate to join the Church *and* the community. It was like an absurd revolution and an amazing revelation! Of course, many persons were already shaping their ministry this way, but now this was actually the stated purpose! Your purpose, or your call, is to link the Church and the world. I found that incredibly liberating. I was no longer limited to the box of Christian educator, or church musician, or the director of (blank) service agency. I can be any and all of those things that my gifts and talents allow with the simple mandate that I work to link the Church and the world." The *mandate,* as this deacon calls it, to link or bridge worship and work gives a unique twist to the service of a deacon.

Just the image of "bridge" is not sufficient, however, to capture the place of the deacon between Church and world. The bridge image may seem static, unchanging, and rigid. The connection that the deacon embodies between worship and work also invites and empowers laity in the work of *diakonia* (service). Deacons are creating bridges of all shapes and sizes. They are responding as God invites and enables the imaginations of deacons and laity.

Another deacon, whose ministry is in "building bridges between God's children who can hear and those who cannot" as a teacher and sign-language interpreter, extends the bridge image: "I picture great bridges that connect God's Church and the world around it. Elders can help ignite a fire, a light to help the people see and learn about God and God's Church, and the life God wishes for us to have in and with the world. Elders can help illumine part of the path across the bridge into the world. It is the deacon who can share that same light within the Church to help guide people through the Church and then, too, be the lantern bearer to walk *with* the people across that bridge, with God's help, guiding them into the world to do God's work. And, being in the world with the people, the deacon makes the return trips, showing new people the way across the bridge into the Church."

Similarly, a deacon whose ministry is the law writes, "Sometimes I am asked, 'What kind of lawyer are you?' and I reply that I am a 'bilingual lawyer. I speak the language of the law and the language of the Church.' By being fluent in both languages, I can help my churches understand what the law expects of them and I can help either the court or secular opponents or both understand what they can expect from the Church."

Her ministry has focused on helping congregations create environments that are safe for children as well as helping the denomination deal with clergy who have been charged with misconduct. The litigious society in which we live has created a need for the ministry of this deacon that bridges court and Church. Her life has always pointed toward this ministry. "I have heard it said that Christians should live with the Bible in one hand and the newspaper in the other (loosely paraphrased from Zan Holmes in the *Disciple I* video for Session 10 [Nashville: Abingdon, 1987]). That is the kind of bridge image that motivates me. I have always, since I was a little girl in elementary school, wanted to be a lawyer. But I never wanted to be just a lawyer who performed tasks without being involved with real persons to make a difference in their lives. And, I have always wanted to be a minister—but I never wanted to be just a minister who performed rituals without helping real persons and making a difference in their lives. By serving as a deacon in full connection, my daily work makes me a bridge for many persons between what the daily world expects and what their hearts are crying out for. Persons look at me, and the work I'm involved in, and conclude that if I can witness to ultimate sacred beliefs and values everyday, then so can they."

Another deacon writes that her ministry "is to help

equip those who gather on Sunday for their life away from the church building." In fact, our worship leads us "out of the confines of the church building to the community that surrounds us. That is what Jesus did. This is what we must do," writes another deacon.

Many deacons see their work as equipping laity to see their lives as opportunities for ministry. In 1976, the section on "The Ministry of All Christians" was added to the *Book of Discipline.* (This section is found in Part 3 of the 2000 version.) This contains the familiar texts "all Christians are called through their baptism to this ministry" (par. 125) and "As servants of Christ we are sent out into the world . . ." (par. 124).[1] However, the notion that ministry is the work of all Christians remains unknown and unrealized for many United Methodists, as the following examples make clear.

- A church asked an active member who had served on the Council on Ministries and Staff-Parish Relations Committee to become chair of the Administrative Council. He replied that he would have to say no to this invitation to ministry, even though ministry was important to him, because the bank where he was employed had added to his workload. The bank had asked him to head up a project that would renovate several downtown hotels into low-cost living spaces for homeless persons. He did not see the bank project as ministry because it was not taking place in the Church or being sponsored by the Church. Deacons equip when they help laity to name their work in the world as ministry, taking Christ to the world in acts of compassion and justice. Another deacon we interviewed describes his work as "widening the scope of God's vineyard." Deacons who work in congregations, such as these, think of the bridge they build connecting the people of the Church with ministry needs in the world.

- A deacon who serves in a Conference-level position says that his goal is "to bridge the structures of the Church with the people who are trying to navigate in what are often uncharted waters for them." His work focuses on removing barriers that might prevent persons from fulfilling their call to ministry.

- "It's hard to bridge worship and work. Last year, I was on a [mission trip] in Haiti. We were making classroom furniture—humbling because my skill set doesn't include carpentry. I'm still pondering how I can make a difference in the world, and how I can help equip those who gather on Sunday for their life away from the church building." She is expressing the worry that plagues many deacons—that their efforts to bring Christ to the world are so small.

- One of our students who is preparing for the ministry of a deacon also wrote of his experience on a mission trip to Haiti. He found himself overwhelmed by the poverty he saw. There was so much need. He was in Haiti for only a few weeks. He could do so little. "It's like trying to move a mountain with a spoon," he said. But he has come to see the importance of what he does and to celebrate it. Now he affirms, "But at least I have a spoon!" Deacons must come to grips with both the immensity of the world's need for ministries of compassion and justice and the finite nature of the work they can do. Otherwise there is despair.

Bridging Relationships Among Ministries

Many functions are needed if the Church is to fulfill its mission. Attempting to clarify the differences in responsibility for ministry, the *2000 Book of Discipline* asserts that while "all Christians are called to minister wherever Christ would have them serve and witness in deeds and words that heal and free" (par. 105), some persons "respond to

God's call by offering themselves in leadership as ordained ministers" (par. 301). The *2000 Discipline* attempts to define all ministry as part of the organic whole.

Thomas Frank, of Candler School of Theology, in his study of United Methodist polity, suggests that United Methodists set aside some for ordination primarily for the "sake of good order." He also notes that "the ordained are set apart for a specialized ministry, but remain part of the people of God. . . . In common with all the people of God, 'specialized' ministers have a calling by the power of the Holy Spirit."[2]

In keeping with the goal of good order, the *2000 Discipline* seeks to describe the functions of the Order of Deacons and the Order of Elders without limiting the power of the Holy Spirit to call persons to ministries that make disciples. It states that those ordained as deacons lead in the ministries of service and "equip others for this ministry through teaching, proclamation, and worship and . . . assist elders in the administration of the sacraments." Those ordained as elders preach and teach the Word of God, administer the sacraments, order the Church for its mission and service, and administer the *Discipline* (par. 303.2).

Regretfully, these words do not make clear distinctions. How is equipping for the ministries of service, a responsibility assigned to the deacon, different from ordering the Church for its mission and service? For the deacons with whom we have spoken, the answer is that the ministries of elders focus on the Church and its task, even those tasks in the world, while the ministries of deacons are located in the world or in bridging Church and world.

In practice, this distinction does not cleanly hold up, but it points to an essential difference in focus. The ministry of the deacon is not to be apart from the world but must not be apart from the Church either. The deacon stands with one foot on each side, creating a bridge between worship and work.

Theologically, this might seem to suggest a duality, a split between sacred and profane. On the contrary, the ministry of the deacon is a testimony to the sacramental nature of all creation. It points to the essential unity of the call of the Church to embody ministry in the world. The ministry of the deacon declares our conviction that God's grace is mediated through the embodied stuff of creation and our lives. "God's redemptive love is realized in human life by the activity of the Holy Spirit, both in personal experience and in the community of believers" (*BOD* par. 101). The sacramental points through the concrete of the here and now to the hidden and invisible God.

As Dwight and Linda Vogel note in their book, *Sacramental Living*, "The sacramental is embodied and present in the world we experience—it is immanent. At the same time, the sacramental opens for us the mystery of God who is beyond all our experience—it is transcendent."[3]

For instance, the simple act of setting a bowl of soup or piece of bread before a hungry person is sacramental. God is present in the act of compassion at the same time that the act points to the God of love who is beyond.

Through acts of compassion and justice, Christ is brought to the world. The ministries of deacons on behalf of The United Methodist Church testify to the worth of all humanity and the healing, reconciling power of Christ in the world. Where compassion, justice, and love bring healing, reconciliation, and life, there is Christ. The responsibility of the deacons is to see that the faith of the community becomes active in deeds of love.[4] As Liv Berit Carlsen, a deacon in The United Methodist Church of Norway, writes, "We are the hands of Christ."[5]

This description of the ministry of the deacon raises the question of the ministry of the laity. There is but one ministry in Christ, but there are diverse gifts and evidences of God's grace in the Body of Christ (Ephesians 4:4-16). The primary focus of the ministry of all the people of God is in the world. The ministry of all Christians is complementary. No ministry is subservient to another. All United Methodists are summoned and sent by Christ to live and work together in mutual interdependence. Guided by the Spirit, "all Christians . . . are called to minister wherever Christ would have them serve and witness in deeds and words that heal and free" (*BOD* par. 126).

Frank, however, suggests that the assertion of complementarity in this paragraph is unsatisfactory because it neglects to identify what is complementary to what! "The jarring note of tension remains; 'no ministry is subservient to another.' "[6] Is this about laity and clergy? Clergy and laity? Or deacons and elders? We need to continue reflecting on the wholeness of ministry. Although all Christians are called to ministry, who we are and what we will do take many forms. The intent of the *Discipline* is undoubtedly to abolish hierarchies and power imbalances. Yet, the relationships remain in tension.

We must explore options of understanding and practice and seek to heal the divisions and misunderstandings between laity, deacons, and elders. Yet, the image of bridge is empowering.

The notion of the sacramental character of all ministry, both at the table and extending the table, may help to reaffirm the organic nature of ministry. No one serves single-handedly bringing the creation into the will of God. Paragraph 303.2 of the *Discipline* states that the deacon will "lead in service" and "equip others for this ministry." Other verbs used in describing the ministry of the deacon are *exemplify, articulate,* and *embody.* By leading, articulating, and embodying the ministries of service to which all Christians are called, deacons can create the conditions where laity are empowered to answer God's call to service and live out their own ministries of compassion and justice.

Although the *Discipline* does not address issues of power, the notion of laity empowered by the leading of deacons is important. To speak of empowerment is to admit that there is power. Power must be considered as we identify the three forms of ministry—laity, deacon, and elder. The disciplinary statement that the ministry of all Christians is complementary on the one hand may refer to the power of each within the Church to make decisions and to expend its resources. On the other hand, the power may be God's grace. Maria Harris reminds us that, "no longer is the pastoral office the only locus of power. Instead, by reason of baptism and confirmation all have been given the power that resides in the grace of the Christ: the power to heal, to remember, to bless; the power to do justice and love mercy and walk humbly with God. In all of us resides the power to be poor in spirit, to be merciful, and to mourn. In all of us resides the power of vocation, of mission, and of ministry."[7] Laity are *empowered*, then, only through the grace of God. The potential power is already present. The deacon leads and equips laity for service, thereby assisting them to share in the power of vocation, mission and ministry.

Deacons as People with Two Languages

Every deacon who is ordained must satisfy The United Methodist Church that he or she has learned theological language. Academic preparation includes either a theological master's degree or the alternate basic graduate theological studies. But every deacon must also satisfy the Church, through the Conference Board of Ordained Ministry, that he or she has another language or set of skills with which to address the needs of the world. This is what makes it possible for the ministry of the deacon to bridge Church and world. The lawyer bridges Church and world because she is proficient in the language of the court as well as the language of the Church. The teacher bridges Church and world because he brings theological understanding to the processes of teaching and learning in the Church. The sign language teacher brings the Church to the hearing impaired as well as the gifts of the hearing impaired to the Church. The bridge-building nature of the ministry of the deacon is made possible because of the dual language or skills that the deacon offers. And the bridge is built because the deacon expressly focuses on that effort.

This is the place of the deacon in The United Methodist Church: to be a bridge between the needs of the world and the ministries of the Church, to help others to cross the bridge from Church to world and from world to Church, and to equip the people of God to be bridge builders who bring the grace and healing and justice of God to the hurting and wounded world.

CHAPTER SIX

The Order of Deacons: A Communal Identity

Deacons have a heightened sense of community with one another. The newly formed Order of Deacons in Iowa met for a retreat. Every ordained deacon in the Conference was present! One hundred percent attendance! They came together with joy. They shared the spirit of "a deacon's heart" and knew that being together would strengthen their ministry through mutual support.

This enthusiasm for the order is not universal, however. The survey of deacons conducted by the General Board of Higher Education and Ministry in 1997 and 1998 found that only 16 percent of deacons listed the Order of Deacons as a major source of support.[1] This may be because most Annual Conferences had not yet organized the order. In many Annual Conferences the formation of the order has been slow and difficult. One deacon whose ministry has been counseling and working with young adults said, "I don't need the community. I have never suffered. I never shared the pain [of injustice or lack of employment]. I think I have more in common with elders."

With the creation of the ordained deacon in full connection, the 1996 General Conference declared that each Annual Conference should have an Order of Deacons and an Order of Elders. The Conference decreed that every ordained person in the denomination would be part of a covenant community "to mutually support, care for, and hold accountable its members for the sake of the life and mission of the church. These orders, separately or together, seek to respond to the spiritual hunger among clergy for a fulfilling sense of vocation, for support among peers during this stressful time of change in the Church, and for a deepening relationship with God" (*BOD* par. 311).

Annual Conferences scrambled to respond to this decree. Each bishop convened the deacons of the Conference to elect a chairperson. The order was quickly organized in some Annual Conferences, and other Annual Conferences took two or more years to get underway. The groups defined their purpose and method of operation according to their understanding of the Disciplinary statement quoted above. Thus, the order takes shape differently from Conference to Conference.

The notion of a covenantal relationship to an order that defines spiritual disciplines for United Methodist clergy is new. However, ordination has always been tied to membership in an Annual Conference. In The United Methodist Church, clergy are appointed to a church but do not become members of that church. Instead, clergy are *members* of the Annual Conference. Thus, clergy in The United Methodist Church have long been accustomed to thinking of their community as the Annual Conference. Moreover, the notion of a covenantal community supporting persons on the spiritual journey is at the heart of the Methodist movement. Classes, bands, and covenant discipleship groups have all been intrinsic parts of the Methodist understanding of the means of grace and support.[2]

The Annual Conference is the occasion to come together each year to report and celebrate what has been accomplished in the year past. It is the opportunity for all—equal representations of clergy and laity—to make plans for the missional work of the year to come. The

Conference debates and votes on resolutions that express opinions on matters of both Church and world. The Annual Conference closes with the ritual "fixing of appointments." This formalizes the agreement by which clergy members of the Annual Conference are sent to serve the missional needs of the Church. For United Methodist clergy, the pattern is to meet to "conference," to worship, celebrate, grieve, and covenant together regarding the work of the year to come, before leaving for another year of service. The home base remains the Annual Conference.

Since 1996, the covenant of United Methodist clergy with the Annual Conference takes two forms. First, it means that a United Methodist clergyperson is in a covenantal relationship to the Annual Conference, agreeing to serve the missional needs of the Church as appointed by the bishop. The 1996 General Conference decided that, because the new deacon would relate to the Annual Conference so differently from elders, each group needed to organize into a separate order. Thus, second, the clergyperson is in a covenantal relationship with the order, which is primarily related to nurturing spiritual growth. Although the *1996 Discipline* states that elders and deacons are accountable to their order, the authority for that accountability is not yet clear. How is it distinct from one's accountability to the Annual Conference? Without further clarification, these dual covenants seem to overlap and may create ambiguity in loyalties.

The covenant with one's order is also new for elders. The number of elders compared to deacons in each Annual Conference is quite large. Though in many cases orders for elders have met to organize, they struggle to define their purpose. Many Annual Conferences have annual pastors' schools or annual daily gatherings that have been occasions for continuing education and spiritual renewal. How the meetings of the order are different from these sorts of occasions is still unclear.

Community of Deacons

Deacons seem to have found it easier to conceive of and connect to their order, perhaps because community was important for their predecessor form of ministry, diaconal ministry. The diaconal ministry was initiated by the 1976 General Conference. The new section of the *1976 Discipline* on the Ministry of All Christians, which stressed the calling of all baptized to a life of service, also created the diaconal minister. This office created a place in the Church for those persons whose specialized ministry was essential to the functioning of many large churches and Conference staffs.

The diaconal minister was a layperson, called by God and gifted for a specialized ministry. These persons were, after proper candidacy processes and academic preparation, consecrated for a lifetime of service to the Church through the specialized ministry. They remained laypersons. Yet, their status in the Church was different. Many spoke of this new office as "neither fish nor fowl" since the diaconal minister was not clergy, but had been set apart from the laity for specialized ministry.

Perhaps because of the ambiguity of their position, diaconal ministers tended to feel a kinship with one another that was important and meaningful. Being a diaconal minister required constant interpretation to laity and clergy alike. Diaconal ministers had no guarantee of an appointment and few safeguards either. They nurtured and supported one another in formal and informal ways and they sought to find their way through the structures of The United Methodist Church.

Diaconal ministers often felt that they had made a commitment to serve in the ministries of the Church but that the Church had made little or no commitment to them. One, who chaired the Board of Diaconal Ministry in his Conference, reported that he had to remind the district superintendent, "Don't leave us out!" Yet, he also expressed frustration with the diaconal ministers who sometimes seemed to choose to be victims of the Church's inattention. "If you want to be recognized, do something that's recognizable," he said with frustration. "I started saying to the cabinet, 'You need to meet with diaconal ministers.' " He was seeking to help the cabinet to recognize the missional potential in the skills and commitments of the diaconal ministers of the Conference. In turn, he emphasized to the diaconal ministers, "You have to be accountable to the cabinet."

Regrettably, every gathering of deacons that we have taken part in over the last two years has seemed to begin with complaining about the lack of understanding and acceptance that deacons have found in the Church. Dr. Sondra Matthaei, of St. Paul School of Theology, puts it succinctly: "Stop whining." Some deacons appear to be stuck in a negative relationship with the authority of the Church.

Others, however, treasure their connection with one another. The deacon who teaches the hearing impaired stressed the importance for her of the Order of Deacons. "You're the only support people I would say that I have—support for what I believe in." Her employment in a public school setting means that those at work, even laity with a high sense of call to ministry, do not also share her accountability to the ministry of The United Methodist Church. Only in the Order of Deacons does she find others whose ministry is bridge building, who are ordained to the ministry in The United Methodist Church, and who are accountable to the Church.

Those who became the first ordained deacons under the *1996 Discipline* all made the transition from serving as a diaconal minister to ordination and service as an ordained deacon. Thus, their bond was already present. As they had struggled to help the Church see the need for the ordained deacon and then attempted to discern whether their own calling was to that new order these persons often remained bonded to one another. One deacon who had been very active in proposing legislation, which led to the permanent Order of Deacons, told this story: "I learned that the ministry study had passed during the last General Conference by calling the toll-free number and listening to a recording. I surprised myself by crying, all by myself, for a very long time. I was overwhelmed that change finally had come, after years of waiting. I was struck, too, by the irony of hearing the news alone, when working for change had been such a corporate task."

She speaks with passion of the connection many diaconal ministers felt after twenty years of struggling to define and help the Church discern the value of this ministry.

Those who are most enthusiastic about the power of the order to undergird their ministry are those who made the transition from the lay office of diaconal minister to the ordained Order of Deacons. "We have all been laity together. It may not be the same when we incorporate new people who have never been diaconal." Those who did not share in the struggle to help the Church envision an ordained deacon will come to the ministry differently. Merging these people into a covenanted order may prove difficult.

The need for community is partly because of the need for accountability, and partly because of the need for support. The community also expands one's understanding of ministry. One deacon writes, "Two years ago I attended the DIAKONIA Conference in Germany. I felt a part of a community that I had only dimly realized existed. The events of the last few years, both in the Church and within my personal life, have led me to a heightened awareness of the global quality of our lives and ministries."

At an ecumenical gathering of deacons, diaconal ministers, and deaconesses, a Lutheran woman said, "Even when I go to a meeting of Episcopalian deacons and walk into a room where I do not know anyone, I feel at home. I know we share the 'deacon's heart.'" The "deacon's heart" is a desire to serve. The heart of a deacon shares a solidarity with all the people of God in the grit and grace of their lives. Ordination as a deacon is an offer to serve the mission of the Church according to one's gifts and graces. It is a covenant with other deacons to seek to work with God toward the healing and reconciling of the creation.

A United Methodist deacon working in conflict resolution spoke of her new "sense that this is what *the Church needs,* not only what I need" (italics added). Her role models are the biblical narratives of those whose names were changed when they responded to God's urgent call to ministry. For instance, Jacob demands a blessing from God and receives it. But his name is changed to Israel and he walks with a limp through the rest of his life. Israel means "he who strives with God" and Jacob bears the mark of that striving. Those who had been diaconal ministers also strove with God as they sought to discern whether God was calling them to be ordained. With ordination, their name changed and they were marked, not with a limp but with the new name: ordained deacon.

Other deacons have found it difficult to relate closely to the order because their work is so unique. One says, "I am a one-of-a-kind deacon and I haven't tried to be too involved or to have too many expectations of the order in terms of my particular work. It seems to me the order needs to form with the needs of most deacons in mind, rather than just mine. Then, I'll tag along when I can."

Her commitment to the ministry of the deacon is unquestioned but she has not yet found the order helpful. However, her sense of the need for accountability and community is undimmed. "I do have two or three individual deacons with whom I frequently share. I think we help one another stay focused in our ways of serving."

The Order of Deacons may teach us all how to share and support one another as we engage in very different ministries. If this can occur, a tremendous contribution has been made to the whole Church because each local congregation of the Church needs to learn how to support the people of God in their very different vocational callings and ministries.

The Order of Deacons in one Conference meets monthly. They report that they "come to this ministry from five different backgrounds: different states, different Conferences, different certifications, different routes into ordination, and different specialties of service." Yet, they are "united by the common calling of connecting the world and the Church." Their different skills and contexts of ministry provide rich conversation as they gather as the Order of Deacons, accountable to one another and to the Church.

Conference Leadership and the Order of Deacons

The shift from diaconal ministers (a lay consecrated office in the Church) to ordained deacons is not without its struggles. Diaconal ministers were clearly set apart from laity by their consecration. Groups of diaconal ministers in each Conference tended to gather together at Annual Conferences and provide leadership during the balloting for lay delegates to the General and Jurisdictional Conferences. The evidence of this is that thirty-two diaconal ministers were elected to the 1996 General Conference and about half that many to the Jurisdictional Conferences. The newly ordained deacons, separated from their lay colleagues (diaconal ministers) for balloting, were slightly less organized and less effective. Thus, just twelve deacons were delegates to the 2000 General Conference and eleven to Jurisdictional Conferences. However, seven diaconal ministers were delegates to the General Conference and two to Jurisdictional Conferences. About six deacons and four diaconal ministers were reserve delegates. Although it is slightly less than the total for 1996, a significant number were on delegations for 2000.

The newly ordained deacons experienced some discomfort with their status as clergy in the political arena of the Annual Conferences. One deacon told us that after she was ordained she began sitting with the elders who are appointed to the same Charge. She felt "lost in the crowd at Annual Conference," which was not a good feeling! Others who had formed close alliances with various lay organizations as diaconal ministers found that they had lost their connections and thus their bargaining power when they could no longer vote for lay delegates to General Conference.

What Would an Order Look Like?

Those ordained as deacons in The United Methodist Church begin with a response to God's call and a recognition of the world's woundedness. The call is experienced individually. Each person must come to the recognition that the call is "for me." But then the journey becomes the responsibility of the whole community of the Church. The journey shifts. It is the whole community that must validate the call, recommend the candidate for ministry, prepare the candidate for ministry (through the candidacy process of the Annual Conference and the academic preparation in the graduate theological schools of the denomination), and test the character and calling of the candidate through the probationary years. The community of the ordained in the Annual Conference ultimately acts on the request for ordination, approving or disapproving those who wish to become a part of their Conference.

The membership in an order, then, is the fulfillment of the commitment to community that is a part of the entire process leading to ordination. The order holds deacons accountable. Deacons must find ways to gather that include times for confession and celebration, for challenge and praise. We confess that God's kin(g)dom is not yet fully realized. Much work of healing and justice and reconciliation remains to be done. Yet we celebrate the glimpses of grace and glory that are part of our ministries. God's love is reconciling and transforming. God is making all things new. Deacons (like elders in their order and laity in covenant groups) need to tell one another these stories of falling short and of success, of the needs of the world and of the opportunities to meet needs that we have experienced. Like Samuel, we announce, "Here I am, Lord!" Thus, we call one another to greater commitment to the work of the kin(g)dom as we celebrate the work that we have done.

The meeting of the order must be supportive. The Order of Deacons is small and often misunderstood. ("It's been that I could step outside the box, knowing that I had people who would say 'Go for it!' ") Most deacons have found a place to serve God and the Church that is satisfying and fulfilling. ("I know that I am where God wants me to be.") But some struggle to find acceptance in the Church. Some are not able to find a way to serve that fulfills their calling and feeds their families. For these and others who are not in the right place yet, the order is a critical support system. For those who are more satisfied that they are in the place of most potential, the meeting of the order is a time for reaffirmation of their gifts and calling that energizes for the work ahead. ("It is such a privilege to serve as a deacon. My sisters and brothers renew my calling and send me back to my work with energy and focus.")

The work is the *raison d'être* of the order. The order exists to help the people of God who have accepted a call to be ordained as deacons carry forward the mission of the Church. The bottom line is the mission of the Church. The order in each Annual Conference must be organized so that it contributes to the mission of the Church by holding deacons accountable to that mission even as it supports them and their ministry.

Examples of Orders of Deacons

Conferences report a variety of organizational plans and goals for the order. For instance, the deacons of the Minnesota Annual Conference expressed a desire for a prayer life, for community, and for opportunities to be in mission together.[3] The Virginia Annual Conference has agreed to "order our lives so as to move closer to union with God and to create a bond of unity and common commitment to mission and ministry." They seek to "hold one another accountable." Clearly, the seventeen deacons in full connection in 1998 were seeking community with one another. Likewise, as we mentioned at the beginning of this chapter, the Iowa Conference deacons met for their first retreat in 1999 and reported 100 percent attendance! The hunger for community within the order brought them together.

The Central Texas Annual Conference formed their order April 21, 1998. These deacons covenanted to "an order grounded in hospitality, where we experience mutual support through community, communion, and communication." They have continued to gather several times a year. Their chairperson reports, however, that meeting as an order has been a "big challenge." Some persons have made it a priority and the retreats have been productive for them. But because of all the demands on their time, others have not attended.

The Order of Deacons in the Baltimore-Washington Conference offers a model for how an order can live out its community values. This group has decided to use retreat times to act on their convictions about building bridges between Church and world. In November 1999 they chose to spend their time together traveling to the community of Blairton, West Virginia, "to stand in solidarity with both the local United Methodist Church and residents of the community as they continue their struggle under the hand of a big corporation."[4]

They learned of this company town in their Conference that was struggling to survive after the company, which had provided employment and services, had to leave the area. The large company was threatening to close access to the town's water supply, which it owned, since it no longer had a presence there. The deacons agreed "to live, even if but a brief time, in the reality of the poor and oppressed. Our motivation was not to go and 'do/fix' but 'go and be.' We wanted to say with our presence 'you are our sisters and brothers in Christ. What is happening to you is unjust and oppressive. We come to walk in solidarity with you. We come to be, not do. We come as servant ministers and we will be pleased to serve you in whatever ways you might find helpful.' "

The deacons met with members of the community to learn how the impasse between the corporation and the community had come to be. The Order of Deacons, concerned for the people in this small town should they lose their access to clean water, decided to join in a quiet demonstration, which resulted in the company agreeing to continue providing water.

The deacons were accountable to one another as they "spoke of the growth in our lives and ministry as deacons called into the world. Our doing so was not a show-and-tell, but accountability." After three days in the community, which included worship, a Charge Conference, and some community cleanup, the deacons were renewed. They stated it this way: "We were all of one accord. We felt that we were truly immersed in the reality of the Blairton church and community. We did feel the people's pain, as well as their joy, and felt that our standing beside them helped to lift the burden. It is amazing what God can do just by assuring people that they are loved."

This model of retreat, immersion, and action apparently was deeply meaningful to its participants. "It offered us insight into who and whose we are, brought us closer to each other, and allowed us to be God's presence in that [community]."

Conclusion

The purpose of an order is not entirely clear from the statement in the *Discipline*. What does it mean to mutually support, care for, and hold accountable persons who are ordained and thereby part of an order? The chairperson of one order reports that deacons in her order struggle to know whether they should focus on spiritual discipline and nurture or whether organizing for tasks such as electing a deacon to General Conference is appropriate as work of the order. Either of these activities provides mutual support. A prayer retreat with the order is support for a deacon. A representative at the General Conference who knows your concerns and votes for your issues is support for a deacon. The language of the *Discipline* is not specific and leaves the activities of an order open to wide varieties of interpretation.

The order, as conceived by General Conference, appears to make the deacons accountable to one another and to the Church. Several deacons envision an order that enables and energizes the deacons to be change agents in the Church. "As a member of the Order of Deacons I can seek to be leaven in the Church, seeking to call the Church to less hierarchical and more compassionate and just ways." As another deacon wrote, "We are sent out, as deacons of The United Methodist Church, to be change agents, not just in the world, but also within the Church."

CHAPTER SEVEN

Partnership: Deacons, Elders, and Laity

A deacon in a large midwestern city directs an agency focused on meeting the needs of women and children caught in the web of poverty. Her ministry brings laity to the agency's community center to tutor children in an after-school program. Laity also teach nutrition to young mothers. They assist clients through the maze of regulations in health care and welfare benefits. Women learn skills so that they are self-supporting. This deacon's ministry brings a loving face of the Church to ministries of service and justice. But it also brings the face of Jesus to the laity who volunteer in the work of the center. "Truly I tell you, just as you did it to one of the least of these who are members of my family, you did it to me" (Matthew 25:40). The people's experiences affect their understandings of God, of the meanings of love and service, and of their calling as Christians.

This deacon also speaks to the Annual Conference and to many church groups, interpreting the work of the center. As she tells the stories of the clients they serve, she bridges Church and world, bringing the needs of the world into the gathered community of faith. These congregations respond with both their financial support and their service. "My agency," says this deacon, "is an arm of the Church. My ministry is an opportunity to make the sermon come alive in the lives of people in this city."

The *Book of Discipline* begins the section on ordained ministry by reiterating that ministry is the responsibility of the whole Church. All persons are called by Christ to "follow in the way of love and service" (par. 301). This call is for all Christians.

However, with Acts 6 as the model, the *Discipline* describes a pattern that divides the work of the ordained ministers of the community. "Those who respond to God's call to lead in service and to equip others for this ministry through teaching, proclamation, and worship and who assist elders in the administration of the sacraments are ordained deacons" (*BOD* par. 303.2). The ordained elder's work is described as "preaching and teaching the Word of God, administration of the sacraments, ordering the Church for its mission and service, and administration of the *Discipline* of the Church" (par. 303.2). These descriptions do not make clear the distinction between the two orders except that elders "administer" the sacraments and deacons "assist." The description of the early Church from Acts 6 does, however, suggest a pattern where some are more focused on the gathered community, with a responsibility to preach, to teach, to administer the sacraments, to nurture, to heal, to gather the community in worship, and to send them forth in witness. Others in this pattern were said to focus more outward: "to care for the physical needs of others, reflecting the concerns for the people of the world" (par. 302).

The two ways of describing a differing focus for ordained ministry are not, however, adequately differentiated. In reality, the work of the elder, even when primarily based in congregational life, hopes to help all Christians understand their calling to make disciples and carry the gospel into all the world. This work then does not simply turn inward. Also, the work of the deacon, teaching and leading, often takes place primarily in the life of a congregation in the role of minister of music or Christian educator. To draw a line between Church and world to differentiate elder and deacon is to create a false dichotomy. In addition, the work of these ordained persons, both elder and deacon, is similar to the work of all Christians, with the exception of the administration of the sacraments, which has been reserved for the ordained elder.

Thus, the decision to ordain deacons in full connection has challenged The United Methodist Church in several ways. Two of the primary challenges are: (1) the creation of two orders of ordained ministry requires that the ministry of the elder be more clearly defined, and (2) the decision requires that the ministry of the laity be defined as well, in relationship with the ministry of deacons and elders.

This chapter, using the experiences of deacons, will argue that elders, deacons, and laity all have roles to play in service to the will of God in seeking healing and reconciliation. Laity, elders, and deacons serve God and Christ best when they are partners in ministry. We will begin with concerns that have been expressed by the deacons, move to how they see themselves working with elders and laity, and end with a description of a mutual ministry.

Concerns Expressed by Deacons

Concern 1:
The ministry of the laity might be devalued

Boards of Ordained Ministry often raise the question to candidates for ordained deacon, "How is the work you will do as a deacon different from that done by laity?" After all, many deacons work at "jobs" that might also be held by laypersons. Barbara Brown Taylor, recognized as one of the most effective preachers in America, faced this concern as she graduated from seminary.

103

If the purpose of the church was to equip all God's people for ministry to the world . . . then it made no sense to designate one of those people "the minister" in a congregation. Likewise, if that person's job was to support members of a congregation in their ministries to the world, it made no sense to set that person "apart" in ordination and then give that person an office inside the four safe walls of the church.[1]

While fraught with potential and possibility, this new order also brings dangers. We could devalue the ministry of the laity and leave it to "professional" deacons. We could create levels of hierarchy where we long for mutuality and partnership. We could lose the unique callings and gifts of deacons by using them to meet the needs of a declining Church and increasingly secular world.

Taylor's struggle with the purpose of ordination and its potential to undermine the ministry of all God's people is right on target. The deacon who is a social worker, serving in a hospital, for instance, could be a layperson and hold the same position. When The United Methodist Church identified diaconal ministry as a lay ministry, many diaconal ministers found themselves easily forming alliances with laity in the Annual Conference. To be able to say, "I'm like you. Let's do this together," made the diaconal minister a partner with laity. Leading laity in ministry for the world is still the responsibility of the deacon, as it was for the diaconal minister. But ordination sometimes puts up a barrier to partnership that is difficult to overcome. Deacons must guard against any sense of elitism. Each deacon must see that her or his ministry is a gift of the Holy Spirit done on behalf of the Church as a primary representation of the love of Christ. The deacon is a part of the whole people of God with a particular role to play, no better than any other role.

One deacon offered a particularly apt metaphor for this notion by combining "light" and "bridge." She wrote of her ministry with hearing impaired persons as a bridge between Church and world: "Elders can help illumine part of the path across the bridge into the world. It is the deacon who can share that same light within the Church to help guide people through the Church and then, also, be the lantern bearer to walk with the people across that bridge, with God's help, guiding them into the world to do God's work. And, being in the world with the people, the deacon makes the return trips, showing new people the way across the bridge into the Church. The ministry of all three—laity, elder, and deacon—is necessary for God's work to be accomplished in the world."

Sharing the light of Christ with the world is the mission of the Church. Laity are the ones who hold the lantern high day after day, bringing the gospel to life wherever they work and live.

Unlike laity, however, the deacon in full connection is strictly accountable to the structure of the Church for this ministry. Although the deacon may be a nurse whose paycheck and annual reviews are coming primarily from the hospital in which he is employed, the deacon/nurse is also accountable to the bishop who must appoint him each year to serve in that way. The accountability is administered through an annual report to the Charge Conference, through the district superintendent and the Board of Ordained Ministry. These accountability structures require that the deacon be reflective about the ministry he offers. He must express his work in theological terms. He must seek continuing education. And he is also appointed to a congregation where he is to serve as leader and participate in worship leadership.

The deacon who is employed as nurse is focused on the ministry of the "job" and accountable to the Church in ways that a layperson is not. The constant requirement to name the work as "the ministry of an ordained deacon" differentiates the orientation of the deacon nurse from the lay nurse. Each of these persons is called to serve God in the ministry of nursing, but the deacon is accountable to the Church in ways the layperson is not.

Taylor struggled for years to understand whether God might be calling her to ordination. She finally realized that she "could pump gas in Idaho or dig latrines in Pago Pago, as far as God was concerned."[2] The critical event for a Christian is baptism. "That is the moment we join ranks with God," writes Taylor. "The decision to become ordained does not supersede that moment; it is simply one way of acting it out, one among very many others."[3] The deacon chooses to act out her or his call from God, marked by baptism, through ordination as a deacon whose ministry is accountable to the Church and makes connections between worship and work, Church and world.

Another deacon, a Christian educator, described her efforts to help her congregation become involved in missional ministries. The children collect food, school supplies, mittens and hats, and toiletries for United Methodist Children's Services in Milwaukee. Adults volunteer in a homeless shelter. But she affirms the centrality of the ministry of the laity: "I firmly believe that the most effective witness comes from those Christian disciples who work in the world—as lawyers, parents, health workers, laborers, farmers, and so forth." Her ministry is to help the people of God claim their work and lives as opportunities to be disciples.

To be servants and disciples of Christ is a responsibility of all Christians. All are called to service *(diakonia)*, not just the deacons. We need to rethink the language of the *Discipline*. In fact, the present use of the term, *servant leadership* in connection with ordination (see *BOD* par. 104) exacerbates the problem. When this language is used for ordination, we have usurped the tasks/ministries of the people of God.[4] Using the language of "servant" for both lay and ordained ministry does not clarify the distinctions, it only makes the distinctions fuzzier.

Concern 2:
The dangers of clericalism and professionalism

Perhaps the greatest danger for the Order of Deacons is that it will either adopt or intensify the hierarchies of clericalism, or both. When deacons become more concerned about their power and position than about the mission of the Church, the order has lost its orientation to *"diakonia"* and thereby, its heart. One deacon wrote with vigor and passion, "These kinds of things concern me: (1) Folks excited about the fantastic vestments they're making/buying, (2) Other folks "haired up" about not being able to do baptisms and communion. We deacons have an equally important sacrament to focus upon—foot washing, and (3) Excitement over the titles on doors and business cards."

She was responding to the tendency of newly ordained deacons to focus on the set-apart status of ordination rather than the calling to service.

Why is she worried about these behaviors? Because she interprets them as actions by persons seeking power and privilege rather than showing concern for serving God and furthering God's work on earth. Ordination has traditionally brought some status. The parson who walked the streets of the village was respected and given certain privileges. The automobile marked "clergy" gets a favored parking spot at the hospital. Clergy are admitted to places where others may not go, such as prisons. An ordained person is treated differently by the Internal Revenue Service and may be eligible for certain tax breaks that are not available to others. A stole may be worn as a symbol of ordination.[5] However, when the deacon's heart remains central to one's identity as a clergyperson, the danger of clericalism is averted.

Concern 3:
The unique ministry of the deacon is confused with the ministry of the elder

In the struggle to make clear the distinctiveness of the deacon, the authority to offer the sacraments is one of the differences often cited. (We discussed this more fully in chapter 4.) Sometimes people speak of the elder as pastor and the deacon as specialized minister. Yet that distinction does not hold up entirely either. One deacon whose ministry is in the world with the poor writes: "I feel like I am a pastor in the larger sense. I am a pastor to the women I teach."

Her pastoral function extends to feeding. "When I'm teaching a class and it's near the end of the month, I tend to bring in a lot more food for snacks because I know that food stamps are running out and the people coming to my class are going to feed their kids first, especially if it's in the summer and the kids aren't at school where they can get their free lunch and free breakfast."

Her pastoral work is different from that of one who pastors a church, but it is pastoral care nevertheless.

Another way that some have sought to clarify the difference between deacons and elders is that deacons are not part of the itinerancy. Elders must covenant to "go where sent" and deacons, who are not guaranteed a place of employment in the Church, must find a place to serve to which the bishop will appoint him or her. But this distinction breaks down as well. For decades now, elders in extension ministries have not itinerated in the strict sense of the word. Some who serve as professors (like Jack), chaplains, and pastoral counselors have found their place of service and sought the approval of the bishop. And deacons (such as Margaret Ann) have itinerated even across Conference lines as they find God's call to new areas of service.

Deacons are part of the leadership available to the

Annual Conference in responding to the missional needs each year. Deacons are appointed by the bishop and cabinet to service. Some bishops approve appointments for deacons in the equivalent of pastoral appointments. Yet deacons have a powerful sense of their specialized gifts and skills. Most deacons feel passionate about serving in ways that honor those gifts and skills. Margaret Ann, for instance, as she considered a move from the ministry of Christian education in the local church to the ministry of teaching in graduate theological education, had to make peace with herself and with God that this new setting for ministry was appropriate for her calling and commitments.

Deacons have a different sense of being equipped to serve the Church by ordination than perhaps those called to general pastoral ministry do. One is a lawyer and will find her place of service appropriate only when it is responsive to those gifts and skills. Another is called to a ministry of healing and presence through chaplaincy. Deacons, with the help of the candidacy process of the Church, have a clear sense of who they are gifted and called to be and how their identity can contribute to the mission of the Church in the world.

As The United Methodist Church has struggled to live into the two orders of ordained ministry, the lines between the distinctive ministries of elders and deacons are sometimes blurred. One deacon expresses his fear of "actions that seem more concerned with privileging elders and keeping deacons in their place than with responding faithfully to needs in the Church and world." She refers specifically to deacons who are asked, for missional reasons, to serve a congregation in a pastoral role. Unless this appointment is clearly interpreted to the deacon, to the congregation, and to the Annual Conference as a response to a missional need in that setting that only that deacon with those specialized gifts can fill, the calling and identity of the deacon have been ignored.

In every Annual Conference where appointments of

deacons to more "pastoral assignments" are contemplated, the ambiguity around the distinctive role of the deacon becomes painful. A deacon in Iowa argues, "Why is it possible for an elder who is a social worker in a hospital setting to remain an elder in extension ministries while deacons are forced to leave our order if we serve as pastor in charge? Why can't there be a parallel list of deacons in congregational ministries? After all, the bishop and cabinet do not have to approve any appointment of a deacon that they believe is not based on the individual deacon's gifts and the congregation's needs."

With the urgency of shrinking clergy pools and charges crying for trained leaders, some Annual Conferences have sought deacons in full connection for appointment to serve as pastors. This makes a certain amount of sense. The deacons in the Conference have much experience with congregational life and know how to construct meaningful worship and teaching contexts in the Church. They are theologically trained. No wonder that some bishops and cabinets have looked to a deacon when making an appointment to a church or charge requiring experienced and skillful leadership. However, these appointments may violate the spirit of the General Conference action in serious ways as they fail to take account of the calling of deacons to specialized ministries that bridge the worship of the gathered community with the world.

The deacon, in his or her heart and authorized calling, is oriented to the Church and the world in ways that are fundamentally different from an elder. To appoint a deacon to a place appropriate for an elder simply because there is no elder available is to violate the sacred trust between the deacon, God, and the Church.

In addition, it reinforces the misconception on the part of some elders that deacons' orders are just "cheap ordination." Those who do not understand the candidacy rigor and academic requirements of the deacon may misunderstand their qualifications to serve in pastoral roles in certain settings. The other side of this same coin is that often deacons do not receive compensation that parallels that received by elders. As one deacon puts it, "I want churches to give salary and benefits in equal portion as elders so we don't become 'cheap pastors!'" We must continue to clarify the distinctions between the ministry of the elder and the ministry of the deacon.

Deacons in Partnership with Elders

"When I heard about that mission project I thought, 'This is deacon and elder working together. I couldn't do it without him. He couldn't do it without me.'" This deacon is serving in a project that includes a new church being planted in a neighborhood of persons who are new residents in the United States. The deacon organizes programs that help people learn about the faith. She trains leaders for those programs. These ministries offer hospitality and the resources of the faith to people who have found themselves in a strange new land. The skills of the deacon complement the skills of the elder who leads worship and offers pastoral care. They are a team.

This is the model for deacon and elder in partnership. Linda Vogel, our colleague at Garrett-Evangelical Theological Seminary, describes a ministry of deacons and elders, side by side, in mutual ministry. "Together we model what it means for each of us to use our unique gifts and calling in ways that honor and build up the Body of Christ." Deacons offer specialized gifts and a sensitivity to certain needs of the world. When elders and deacons work side by side, their ministry can be complementary.

For instance, a deacon in Kentucky, who we mentioned before briefly, teaches life skills to women who struggle to become self-supporting. She is also building a partnership with the pastors of churches in her district. She is able to interpret the needs of the world to them. She helped one congregation see the need for clothes in good condition that these women could wear to job interviews and to work at their new positions. The congregation responded and even included monetary donations for dry cleaning bills. "I got the sizes of women in my current class and was able to take a number of outfits over and one day we had a kind of makeover day. I had somebody come and give the women facials and they all got at least one new professional outfit; it really did make a difference. For somebody's self-esteem who is looking at being a professional, that is a big step forward."

This work has opened her eyes to the specific needs of people in the community and given her insight into which needs churches might meet. She is now "helping churches shape how they want to be involved in the community" because she knows not only the needs of the poor but also the resources of the welfare system. One pastor called because his church was thinking of beginning a neighborhood community center that could offer tutoring, computer skills and so forth to children. "I feel like what I'm doing now has opened my eyes to those kinds of needs," she says, and she is able to help churches shape their response as faithful disciples of Christ. The work of this deacon, in partnership with the elders of her district, is bringing the Church to the world and the world to the Church. She builds bridges between women on the margins and jobs that bring independence, between the Church and the needs of the world, between elders and deacons and laity.

Deacons in Partnership with Laity

"One concern I have is the feeling that some parishioners have given me that *now* I'm a *real* minister. This signals a need for educating my congregation in the ministry of all believers." Finding ways to work in partnership

112

with laity is the crux of the matter for deacons. Their ministry exists to empower and resource the ministry of laity. As a Christian educator puts it, "I am called to offer processes that facilitate hard listening, deep questioning, creative imagining, logical and divergent thinking—all in the service of faithful living." Her expertise is used to create contexts for learning where together the people of God can discern what God is asking of them.

Hopes and Possibilities for Mutual Ministry

The ministry of the deacon creates and enhances connections between the worship of the congregation and the work of laity in the world. Deacons have the potential to clarify, focus, and empower ministry that serves God's purposes in both Church and world. This potential is most fully realized when the deacon is in partnership with both elders and laity and the gifts of the whole people of God are valued and empowered. As The United Methodist Church lives into the newly defined ministry of the deacon, possibilities for mutual ministry in service of God will be discovered.

The theology that undergirds this connection emphasizes the omnipresent God and the possibility for humans to experience God, through our senses and, mysteriously, beyond our senses, both in the ordinary of life and in the mystery that empowers life. The ministry of the deacon has the potential to point to the presence of God both in the world and beyond the world.

How does it do that? The presence of the ordained deacon serving in the realities of life in the world, whether as nurse, teacher, administrator, organizer, or whatever, is an expression of the hope of the Church that God's power and presence is available to transform and reconcile anywhere and everywhere. The ministry of the deacon is also a concrete effort, on behalf of the Church, to begin the reconciliation and healing of creation, which is God's ultimate will. The ministry of the deacon is a signpost to the world that the Church is present and giving energy to the work of justice and compassion. As the *1996 Discipline* states, the "ministry of service is a primary representation of God's love" (par. 303.2). The ministry of the deacon is sacramental, pointing to the mystery of God's presence both in and beyond the day-to-day realities of life.

These theological possibilities and hopes, however, are not all that the ministry of the deacon carries. Because ordaining a person to stand in this intersection of Church and world is new, it remains to be seen what all the implications will be. The ministries of both laity and elders must be clarified anew because of the deacon. In this sense, the new deacon is a leaven in the Church, changing the shape of some old familiar structures and terminology even as it takes the Body of Christ into the world.

The ministry of the deacon, if not held accountable to the Church, could bring some very undesired results. Accountability structures must be clearly defined or deacons might be doing ministry in the name of the Church that the Church would not want to claim. *Keeping the connections tight and the options for contexts of service loose is the key to optimizing the potential of the deacon in full connection to represent God's love in the world.*

The deacon is a leader who bridges Church and world and thus is at the edge of both. Systems theory tells us that change comes from the edge. Deacons therefore are in position to effect change in both Church and world. The deacon as agent for change, listening to the will of God and responding to the needs of the world, presents a hope for tomorrow in The United Methodist Church.

CHAPTER EIGHT

Accountability, Appointments, and Benefits

Jimmy Carr[1]

The authors have wisely mentioned that the deacon in full connection, called to a lifetime of ordained ministry, is a bridge between the Church and the needs of the world and provides opportunities for the concrete incarnation of God in the world. The very nature of the deacon is to lead in a service ministry of all baptized persons toward a just and righteous world.

In order to consider issues of appointment, accountability, clergy status, salary, and benefits, one must take into account three things: (1) the ministry of the deacon will challenge the Church to think and operate in new ways, (2) the Church must treat all persons who serve vocationally, including the deacon, fairly and justly, and, (3) in many instances, the call of the deacon may challenge individuals not to think of themselves first.

Deacons should consider the needs of the world and how their ministry can lead in making better the life situations of the marginalized and dispossessed. Deacons are accountable at every level to the Church that ordains them. Fair appointment practices and compensation are needed and appropriate, but they are not the primary focus leading deacons into their ministries of Word and Service.

Appointment

Primary Appointment

Deacons in full connection can be appointed to a myriad of ministries. According to paragraph 322.1 of the *Discipline,* deacons may be appointed to their primary appointment:

a) Through agencies and settings beyond the local church that extend the witness and service of Christ's love and justice in the world by equipping all Christians to fulfill their own calls to Christian service; or

b) Through United Methodist Church-related agencies, schools, colleges, theological schools, ecumenical agencies; or

c) Within a local congregation, charge, or cooperative parish.

The order of places of service found in the *Book of Discipline* is important because it affirms that The United Methodist Church is open to deacons serving everywhere in the name of the Church, including local churches. The listing of appointment possibilities indicates that even though deacons can serve in United Methodist agencies, schools, local congregations, cooperative parishes, or ecumenical agencies, an enhanced emphasis is on the service of the deacon beyond the local church. No appointment is too unusual for deacons if certain conditions are met. The place of service must clearly be directed to Word and to spreading Christ's love and justice. Deacons do not merely see their work as personal and private, but also as an opportunity to equip and call the baptized to live their lives in service to Christ through word and deed.

The ministry of the deacon is progressive polity for the ordained clergy in The United Methodist Church. In the past, ordained persons served the Church mostly in local congregations. If they served beyond the local church they were assigned often with limited encouragement and support from the wider Church. Elders in extension ministries are appointed "to serve in ministry settings beyond the local United Methodist church in the witness and service of Christ's love and justice" (*BOD* par. 334.1). Deacons bring an expanded understanding of appointments beyond the local church. While they extend Christ's love in the world, in so doing they are required to see their ministries as opportunities of equipping all Christians to fulfill their own calls. The equipping nature of the deacon is a further shift in understanding that will increase the expectation of ordained persons to be more conscious of their role in calling, training, and empowering the baptized to be the ministers of the Church.

There are at least three unique characteristics of the appointment of the deacon: (1) the appointment is non-itinerate where in the past all ordained ministers have taken vows to itinerate, (2) deacons, at their request, may be appointed to a nonsalaried position, and (3) all deacons serving outside local congregations also have an appointment to local churches (see *BOD* par. 322).[2]

These unique characteristics exhibit a commitment by The United Methodist Church to ordain persons to serve wherever there is a determined need. Along with this uniqueness is the polity that allows deacons to be appointed to a nonsalary position (*BOD* par. 322.6*d*), to less than full-time settings (par. 322.7), appointed across Annual Conferences (par. 322.8), and appointed to other denominations (*BOD* par. 322.9). This range of possibilities is further evidence of The United Methodist Church's desire to serve wherever there are identified needs.

Care and understanding will be needed to enable a nonitinerate ministry to exist beside an itinerate ministry. The appointment of the deacon can be initiated by the bishop, the deacon, the agencies or local churches (see *BOD* par. 322.6*a*), but a deacon does not have the right to a guaranteed appointment as do other ordained persons (see *BOD* par. 322.14*e*). This too will require interpretation in order to develop a unified ministry among elders and deacons.

Second Appointment

Deacons are required to serve in a second appointment if they serve beyond the local church. For instance, a deacon whose primary appointment is as a campus minister encourages students to worship in The United Methodist Church in the community where he or she has a second appointment. The congregation reaches out to the students and claims their ministry on the campus. They ask students to bring prayer concerns to the congregation's worship and prayer circles. Great energy and enthusiasm for a unified ministry within the congregation and the campus ministry have been generated through the second appointment of the deacon.

Stories of deacons in second appointments like this one are further evidence of the shift in our understanding of the practice of ordained ministry. There is inherent hope of making more effective the ministry of all Christians and inviting local churches to reach out and join in the community ministries of deacons. All deacons have an appointment to a local church. "When deacons in full connection serve in an agency or setting beyond the local church, the bishop, after consultation with the deacon and the pastor in charge, shall appoint the deacon to a local congregation where they will take missional responsibility for leading other Christians into ministries of service" (*BOD* par. 322.4).

Just as the primary appointment of a deacon is reaching out to serve the needs of the community and the world, the second appointment has as its major thrust the missional life of the congregation and the ministries of all its members.

Even though the second appointment is one of the truly unique aspects of the ministry of the deacon, it can also be confusing. Questions arise, such as What processes do deacons serving in a primary appointment beyond the local church use to determine an appropriate second appointment to a local church? What are the responsibilities of the deacon in a second appointment? To whom will they relate in the second appointment? A process has been developed that may be useful to deacons, bishops, and local church pastors as they struggle to make the second appointment meaningful and important to the life of the Church (*BOD* par. 322). Also some are seeking to clarify how deacons can be accountable to the staff-parish committee as they serve within the second appointment.

The second appointment to a local congregation of a deacon serving in an agency or setting beyond the local church has the potential of radically enhancing the understanding of ordained ministry and expanding the missional opportunities and ministries of the Church. The fact that local church pastors have available another pair of hands should not only make more effective the ordained leadership but should enhance the daily ministries of the members. A deacon who serves in a Church agency and is fluent in Spanish was appointed by her bishop to a local congregation with the potential of having a significant ministry with Hispanics in their town. The pastor is elated to have such resources from an ordained colleague who will be able to relate to the Spanish-speaking persons and equip the members of the church to better serve the Hispanic community in the name of Christ.

Tent Making

Nonstipendiary appointments allow the deacon in The United Methodist Church, for the first time, to have tent-making ministries within the ordained clergy. This arrangement will allow deacons who are willing to provide the skills of their livelihood beyond their appointment to consider the need in their community where the services of an ordained leader would be valuable. These appointments have the potential of significantly expanding the ministries and outreach of The United Methodist Church to meet identified missional needs. Nonstipendiary appointments also allow the deacons in The United Methodist Church to be aligned with the order of deacons in the Episcopal and Roman Catholic churches who generally serve in nonstipendiary appointments.

Two stories help illustrate this point. A successful businessperson retired early. Soon she felt God's call in her life to serve the unemployed and homeless with a ministry of assisting persons to find places of productive services in the world. She is now in seminary preparing to become an ordained deacon in full connection. She has told her district committee and district superintendent she will seek ordination and an appointment without a salary or benefits. Another person is an executive with a large insurance company and receives enough compensation for his family through that work. He is an ordained deacon who is appointed to a prison ministry working in the evenings and weekends without a salary or benefits. The apostle Paul would be pleased that these persons have heard God's call and are using all their resources and gifts to serve God in behalf of the Church as ordained deacons, especially without a stipend.

Accountability of a Deacon

The deacon is accountable at every level in The United Methodist Church. "This appointment shall be in a setting that allows one to fulfill the call to specialized ministry and where supervision is provided with goals, evaluation, and accountability acceptable to the bishop, cabinet, and the board of ordained ministry" (*BOD* par. 322.5).

To the Bishop, Cabinet, Board of Ordained Ministry, and Other Clergy

Deacons in full connection are recommended for ordination by the Conference Board of Ordained Ministry and approved by the clergy session in the Annual Conference. Any change in the Conference relationship such as leaves of absence, family, maternity, and disability leaves, or retirement is considered closely by the bishop, district superintendent, and Board of Ordained Ministry. The Board of Ordained Ministry makes recommendations for changes in Conference relationship to the clergy session of the Annual Conference for vote (see *BOD* par. 351-58).

Deacons have the responsibility of clarifying for the board and cabinet how they envision their ministries with regard to the ministry of all the baptized. The *Discipline* states the deacon may be required to provide a "written statement of intentionality of servant leadership" (par. 322.6*b*). Thus, deacons have expectations and limitations on their service in the name of the Church. Bishops and cabinets have the responsibility of working with deacons to determine the advisability and appropriateness of appointments. This is such a serious responsibility that the Ministry Interpretation Committee of the Council of Bishops developed the following questions to assist cabinets:

a) Is the proposed ministry setting one in which the vows of ordination to Word and Service can be fulfilled?

b) Does the proposed setting of ministry provide opportunity to maintain a relationship and accountability with the order and the structure of the Church?

c) Is the proposed ministry congruent with the Church's missional commitment in and to the world?

d) Does the person possess the specific/special gifts, training, education, work experience, and experiences of grace required for the proposed ministry?[3]

Legislation approved by the 2000 General Conference further assisted cabinets and Conference Boards of Ordained Ministry in determining the advisability of certain appointments by asking the General Board of Higher Education and Ministry, through the Section of Deacons and Diaconal Ministries, to provide guidelines to validate the appropriateness in service beyond the local church in special settings and to be available for consultation with bishops and cabinets.

The bishop and cabinet have full responsibility in determining whether deacons are appointed. Even though the deacon is nonitinerant, bishops and cabinets have the authority to refuse appointment of a deacon if it is determined that a particular setting is "not . . . in the best interest of the Church" (*BOD* par. 322.6c). This authority of the bishop along with the lack of guaranteed appointment makes the nonitinerate nature of the deacon more accountable to the bishop. No matter where deacons serve, in a local congregation or settings that extend the ministry of Christ in the world, deacons are accountable to the Church.

All appointments of a deacon "shall be in a setting that allows one to fulfill the call to specialized ministry and where supervision is provided with goals, evaluation, and accountability acceptable to the bishop, cabinet, and the board of ordained ministry" (*BOD* par. 322.5).

When settings do not provide evaluation or accountability as in a self-employed position, a board or advisory committee may be required by the bishop, cabinet, and Board of Ordained Ministry that would ensure proper procedures for supervision and evaluation.

As a Probationary Member

Accountability exists from the beginning for ordained deacons in The United Methodist Church as they are elected to probationary membership and become commissioned ministers. They are appointed by the bishop to a place of service and during the entire time are involved in a probationary program provided by the Conference Board of Ordained Ministry. They are evaluated by the district superintendent and the Board of Ordained Ministry on their ability to give leadership in servant ministry. They must demonstrate effectiveness in ministry (see *BOD* par. 317).

To a Charge Conference

The ordained deacon shall relate to a Charge Conference within the bounds of an Annual Conference in which they hold membership. When the appointment is in another Annual Conference, the deacon will also relate to a Charge Conference where they reside. It would be most appropriate for the Charge Conference relationship to be in the church where the second appointment is held. Charge Conference membership takes place through consultation between the deacon, pastor, Staff-Parish Relations Committee, and with the approval of the district superintendent (*BOD* par. 322.11).

Reporting of a Deacon

All deacons are required to report annually concerning their ministry, work, and goals for the future. These reports are made to the Charge Conference with copies going to the bishop(s), district superintendent, Board of Ordained Ministry, and Conference secretary.

It is imperative the deacon serving outside the local church retain a close relationship to the Annual Conference in order for the Church to celebrate and claim their ministry. Reporting to the Church at every level assists the deacon in visualizing his or her accomplishments in ministry and assists the Church in recognizing the nature of the deacon's ministry in the name of the Church.

"Deacons under appointment beyond the local church shall submit annually to the bishop, and the district superintendent, with a copy to their board of ordained ministry, a written report on the official form developed for the Church by the General Council on Finance and Administration for use by the annual conference.

"This report shall include a copy of the evaluation by the institution in which the deacon serves. The report and evaluation shall serve as the basis for the evaluation of these deacons in light of the missional needs of the church and the fulfillment of their ordination to be minister of Word and Service. Deacons serving in appointments outside the conference in which they hold membership shall also furnish a copy of their report to the bishop of the area in which they reside and work" (*BOD* par. 322.3).

To Staff-Parish Relations Committees

The deacon in full connection is accountable to the Staff-Parish Relations Committee in the local congregation where they hold an appointment (*BOD* par. 258.2).

Whether deacons relate to a local church in either a primary or secondary appointment affects how they connect with the committee. Deacons who have a primary appointment can expect from the Staff-Parish Relations Committee all the support, counsel, and evaluation accorded clergy. Deacons who serve in an appointment outside the local church and are in a second appointment to a local congregation are in a less structured situation in the local church and will need to work with the pastor and the committee pertaining to their relationship and accountability to the congregation.

According to *The Book of Discipline,* the Staff-Parish Relations Committee has the responsibility to confer and counsel with deacons who are staff in order to pursue an effective ministry. It is to keep the pastor and staff advised of conditions affecting ministry and relations between staff and the congregation as well as interpret to the people the nature and function of ministry (par. 258.2*f*).

The committee, further, will "develop and approve written job descriptions and titles"; counsel with the deacon on matters pertaining to his or her relationship with the congregation, including establishing priorities in relation to the goals and objectives set for the congregation's mission and ministry; evaluate the deacon annually for the deacon's use for effective ongoing ministry; and identify continuing education needs and plans based on the criteria established by the Board of Ordained Ministry (see par. 258.2*f*).

Deacons, along with the pastor and other staff, have the right to expect work support and encouragement at every point from the Staff-Parish Relations Committee in order to provide a significant ministry. The deacons can also expect a written statement and policy regarding the process for hiring, contracting, evaluating, promoting, retiring, and dismissing as it relates to them.

Relationships with deacons beginning at the time of appointment and continuing on a regular basis would enhance the second appointments to local congregations. "Deacons [are] accountable to the pastor in charge, the charge conference, and other bodies that coordinate the ministry in the local church" (*BOD* par. 322.4). The Staff-Parish Relations Committee is responsible to make sure there is adequate staff to provide an effective ministry and the deacon in a second appointment should enhance that ministry by participating in the life and mission of the congregation.

Deacon as Clergy

Legislation approved by the 2000 General Conference clearly indicates that deacons in full connection are clergy in The United Methodist Church (see *BOD* par. 140). They have all the rights and privileges of full Conference membership alongside the elders. Deacons are eligible to serve and hold office as clergy on boards, committees, and so forth in the Annual Conference. Deacons are also eligible for election as clergy delegates to the General, Central, and Jurisdictional Conferences (see *BOD* par. 320.2).

Even though The United Methodist Church was clear in its understanding of the clergy status of deacons, it was initially unclear as to how the Internal Revenue Service would classify the deacon for income tax purposes. When the IRS issued a ruling related to clergy status of three deacons, Mary Logan, General Counsel of the General Council on Finance and Administration of The United Methodist Church commented: "We are particularly pleased that the IRS has upheld the denomination's polity about the new Order of Deacon and Order of Elders— both are ordained clergy."[4] The IRS ruling made clearer for all concerned that deacons are considered clergy by the Church and the government. This allows deacons to have a housing allowance or exclude from taxes an amount of salary to pay for housing. Deacons will thus be considered self-employed for Social Security purposes and will pay the total FICA.

Compensation and Benefits

"Deacons in full connection with their primary appointment to a local congregation, charge, or cooperative parish shall receive salary—not less than the minimum established by the Annual Conference for full-time and part-time pastors" (see par. 322.14*a, b*). Deacons who desire to serve in a setting that pays less than the minimum salary may be appointed for less than full time at his or her initiative to serve one-quarter, one-half, or three-quarters' time (see *BOD* par. 329). Local congregations, cooperative parishes, and charges will greatly benefit from the ministries of the deacon in its missional life and should improve the effectiveness of the ministries of its members. Every effort should be made to meet the Conference minimum salary. Bishops and district superintendents can greatly enhance the Church and ministry of the deacon by advocating for equitable salaries.

Deacons serving in settings outside the local church receive their salaries and benefits from their employers and are not under the requirements of the minimum salary set by the Annual Conference.

Deacons are eligible and shall participate either in the Ministerial Pension Plan, Cumulative Pension and Benefit Fund, Comprehensive Protection Plan, or the Personal Investment Plan administered by the General Board of Pension and Health Benefits of The United Methodist Church if they serve in congregations or Church agencies. The pension should be paid by the Church with whatever employer contribution is required. If the employer fails to do so, deacons can pay the entire amount themselves. The 2000 General Conference made it clear that all deacons serving in a "local congregation, charge, or cooperative parish . . . shall participate in the denominational pension and benefit plans, programs, and in the health benefit and supplemental programs of his or her annual conference . . . where health coverage is not provided from another source" (*BOD* par. 322.14*b*).

The present practice is for the local churches, charges, or cooperative parish to pay for these benefits. However, some Annual Conferences that pay for pension and benefits for clergy are giving consideration to including deacons as well. It is only right and just that deacons receive the same benefits as ordained elders. Deacons perform a significant service not only for local churches but also for the larger United Methodist Church.

Conclusion

The Order of Deacons in full connection offers many unique and challenging opportunities for the future. The diaconate has at its very heart the mission and ministry of the Church. Deacons, who are ordained to Word and Service, are committed to make the ministry of all Christians more effective and to eliminate hurt and suffering in the world in the name of Christ. It is right that churches treat deacons with respect, and value them by providing all the support, salary, and benefits possible. Deacons, because of their special call and commitment, enhance the Church's commitment to their ministry by following diligently practices that uphold high ideals of work. The Church and deacons working together can build a stronger future committed to mission and ministry.

CHAPTER NINE

Rethinking Ministry, Church, and Ordination in The United Methodist Church

What are the implications of the stories and understandings we have heard from deacons? How are these emerging realities of the ministries of deacons affecting the Church? Many of those with whom we talked spoke of the significant changes occurring in their own self-understandings as deacons and as leaders in the Church, but they spoke even more of changes occurring in the practices of the churches with which they are involved.

As we have mentioned, conversations about the ministry of the laity seem to have significantly increased in those seminaries where the Order of Deacons is taken seriously. This change in ordering leadership for the Church provides an opportunity for the people of God to rethink the ministry, the Church itself, and ordination. This moment in history may renew the participation of all people of God in ministry and recover baptism as the primary ordination, an ordination to Christian life. We now turn to these areas of potential change and empowerment.

Professionalism and Beyond

We live in a professional culture. Concerns for competence and skill in the delivery of services have created professional societies that monitor the skill and ethics of those who serve. Examples of these societies include the American Bar Association, the American Medical Association, state Boards of Education, and accrediting agencies such as the Association of Theological Schools. Professional members within these societies are licensed only after extensive education and testing, passing bar, medical, or teaching examinations to achieve accreditation. In order for a person to stay in good standing, continuing education is required, as well as the continual monitoring of effectiveness.

Professionals are to have specialized skills and expert knowledge in order to assist and lead others. Furthermore, professionals hold one another to codes of ethics defining boundaries of professional relationships and appropriate behavior. Violation of these codes results in penalty, including possibly the relinquishing of the professional license. At its core, professionalism is concerned with improvement of public service. This professional attitude has also permeated the Church. Here, too, the education of those authorized as leaders is monitored. A code of ethics has been expanded and reinforced.

Nevertheless, professionalism can also result in an esoteric use of language and the creation of a hierarchy. For example, medical schools teach a language of communication for medical workers. Medical language refers to concrete realities in the lives of people. But for outsiders, this language is confusing. Its use inhibits engaged conversation between a patient and medical personnel. A hierarchy of professionals also results with specialists at the top, followed by general practitioners, doctors' assistants, nurses, and medical technicians. Often holistic healers and alternative practitioners are excluded. The profession of medicine has sought to protect itself against these tendencies by seeking to emphasize the whole person, by working on "bedside manner" and communication, and by creating conferences also attended by the patient and his or her family who contribute to medical decisions.

The problems of this culture of professionalism have extended to the Church. A "clerical paradigm" has been created where the clergy are educated in theological knowledge, approaches to interpreting the biblical and theological traditions, and the practices of ministries. The theologian Edward Farley, in the following words, has described the result of this "clerical paradigm":

> Why is it that the vast majority of Christian believers remain largely unexposed to Christian learning—to historical-critical studies of the Bible, to the content and structure of the great doctrines, to two thousand years of classic works on the Christian life, to the basic disciplines of theology, biblical languages, and Christian ethics? Why do bankers, lawyers, farmers, physicians, homemakers, scientists, salespeople, managers of all sorts, people who carry out all kinds of complicated tasks in their work and home, remain at a literalist, elementary-school level in their religious understanding? How is it that high-school-age church members move easily and quickly into the complex world of computers, foreign languages, DNA, and calculus, and cannot even make a beginning in historical-critical interpretation of a single text of Scripture?[1]

Church professionalism can inhibit not only the theological understanding of the people of God, but also the acquiring of the practices of faith formation and Christian service, thus too often restricting the religious discourse of the people of God to piety and morality.

This "clerical paradigm" results in the development of a language to describe the realities of faith that too often becomes the jargon of the professionally trained. In addition, the paradigm creates a hierarchy of ministry where persons are ordered according to function. The congregation hires "professional" church leaders to fulfill all of the functions of ministry from teaching, to care, to ritual leadership, and to service. Laity are bystanders as professionals do ministry.

In contrast, early Methodism was a movement that respected education and effective leadership. It was also a reforming movement within Christian faith seeking to return the shared responsibility for living Christian life to all of the people of God. Wesley reached out to populations who were spurned by other religious groups. Wesley was startled by the power of the Holy Spirit to call people through the Methodist movement to new life and leadership. People, whom others had avoided, found new life, sought growth in faith and understanding, and ministered effectively in the name of God.

The covenantal structure of early Methodism provided a means by which persons could grow in faith and be tested and supported for faithful living in the world. "How is it with your soul?" was the question asked of a group member in the Wesleyan classes and bands as they all sought to grow in faithfulness, discipleship, and vocation.[2]

As the Methodist movement developed in the United States, education for spiritual formation, understanding, and vocation were always key concerns. One of the early actions of the Methodist Book Concern in Cincinnati, Ohio, in the mid-1800s was the creation of a library of books, approximately forty in number, that could be purchased and made available to struggling churches and their members on the frontier. These also supplemented the education of clergy, which was usually conducted as they rode circuits and learned from experienced colleagues.

Methodism has always had a high regard for education. Some of the first support of the Sunday school came from Methodists calling for up to eight hours of instruction on Sundays in Bible and life that assisted the way a child grew in public life. The "course of study" program was developed in the mid-1800s. It assisted clergy in enhancing their skills, education, and faithfulness when only limited seminary facilities were available for the education of pastors. Schools were a fundamental institution of growth and healing, along with hospitals and orphanages, as Methodists reached out in mission in the United States and around the world.

All of these efforts were to assist the people of God in faithfulness and in ministry and service. Methodism has been a movement supporting and encouraging the ministry of all Christians in daily living. Methodism has held together the concerns for professional training of leaders and for the responsibility of all Christians to engage in leadership and service.

For example, Garrett-Evangelical Theological Seminary, the seminary where we both serve, evidences this dual commitment in its core purpose: "To know God in Christ, and, through preparing spiritual leaders, to assist others to know God in Christ." The purpose of the seminary is to assist leaders to grow in the knowledge and service of Christ so that others too may grow in knowledge and service.

This dual commitment is deeply embedded in the soul of Methodism. In fact, in the *Discipline*, immediately following the statement of the doctrinal heritage is the section on "The Ministry of All Christians"; that is, how the theological and social heritage are to be carried out:

> The heart of Christian ministry is Christ's ministry of outreaching love. . . . All Christians are called to this ministry of servanthood in the world to the glory of God and for human fulfillment. . . . (par. 104)
>
> This ministry of all Christians in Christ's name and spirit is both a gift and a task. The gift is God's unmerited grace; the task is unstinting service. . . . (par. 106)
>
> The people of God, who are the church made visible in the world, must convince the world of the reality of

the gospel . . . the church is either faithful as a witnessing and serving community, or it loses its vitality and its impact on an unbelieving world. (par. 107)

Using the image of "the Body of Christ," the Church is described as being composed of people with various gifts and ministries who must work together for the redemption of and service to the world. As servants, the people of God are nurtured by grace and spiritual formation (see *BOD* par. 112-14). These servant leaders *both "lay and ordained* . . . share in the preparation of congregations and the whole Church for the mission of God in the world" (*BOD* par. 115; italics added).

Again and again in the literature and official statements of the Church, both the gifts of all of the people of God and particular efforts to educate persons as spiritual leaders are emphasized. Therefore, the separation of the people of God and professional leaders of the people found in much of contemporary Church life should be resisted. The Church is "a diverse people of God who bring special gifts and evidences of God's grace to the unity of the Church and to society" (*BOD* par. 117).

Baptism, as the extending of God's grace and the call to faithfulness, is, in fact, the primary ordination of all Christians for service and ministry. The Church, in its theological interpretations and practical definitions of order, needs to find language that adequately expresses the inclusivity of ministry and encourages the "ordination" of all Christians through baptism to ministry.

Rethinking Ministry

The experiences resulting from the expansion of ministry in the new Order of Deacons in full connection may provide a stimulus to enlivening the ministry of all Christians. Deacons' lives are bridging the realities of the world with the life of the faith community. Deacons also are experiencing ministries as sacramental, opening windows on the Holy and assisting people to see God in ordinary moments of life.

Therefore, the ministry of deacon creates a bridge that reveals the sacred in the ordinary moments of life, from the care given to a scared, single mother by a *doula,* to the instruction in life skills provided by a faithful servant of Christ in a Kentucky program for community women, to the Christ-representing care given by a lawyer working with child advocates. These ministries, along with those of caring for children, parish nursing, congregational music, teaching, leadership, chaplaincy, and environmental ecology, to name a few, extend the "table" into the world. Like the ministries of the eucharistic table, they witness to the mysterious presence of Christ in the midst of the world, they celebrate and nurture others in the food of faith, and they proclaim the reality of the kingdom of God as a reality in which people can trust. In this way, they are a "bridge" because the reality of the Eucharist found at the table is extended into the world. In addition, through the bridge both theological education and education in understandings and skills of service are highlighted. An appropriate tension is held between the gifts of professionalism and the call of all to be involved in servant leadership in Church and in world.

As authorized servant leaders in the Church, the deacon enlivens the potential holiness of the ministries of the people of God as they seek to live faithfully in their lives of education, healing, care, management, community building and service, advocacy, and public leadership in the world. The deacon, as the elder, is authorized by the Church for service, that is, the deacon is an official representative of Christ's ministry. The deacon is a servant-leader who, as Cardinal Bernardin explains, is a "model" or a "sign." Deacons "inspire, enable, and prepare the laity for the service of others. How faithful the deacon is to his [or her] call will be evident to the extent that others

135

are inspired, welcomed, and led to engage in the ministry of service."[3]

As an *authorized* minister of the Church, the deacon reflects the deep encouragement of the Church for all the baptized to represent how ordinary moments of life may be moments of God's servant ministry for others.

The difference between the deacon and the layperson is the authorization and recognition of the Church and the concomitant responsibility of the deacon to the Church. Through the ministries of the ordained, both actions of laity within the Church to teach, nurture, and build up the faith and within everyday life to live as faithful witnesses to the promises of God's reign are affirmed, encouraged, and empowered.

Moreover, all of the moments of life are potentially made holy. As the Church recognizes and authorizes the servant leadership and representative ministry of a deacon in education, the holy and servant nature of education can be made visible. As the Church affirms and authorizes a deacon engaging in the ministry of counseling, the holy and servant nature of counseling is made visible. As the Church affirms and authorizes the ministry of a deacon in community organizing who is seeking to assist a community in providing a safe and nurturing environment for the people who live within its boundaries, the holiness and servant nature of tasks of leadership and community building are made visible.

These realities are a long-standing part of the understanding of the ministry carried on by the people of God. The recognition and affirmation of the Holy One's presence in ordinary time and of the servant nature of laity responding to the calling of vocation have a long history. Yet, with the creation of the Order of Deacons in full connection, with reflection on this new reality in the Church, and with the concrete recognition of how the Church can expand the ministries of the table, we are at a transitional time when the ministries of all Christians can be seen anew and renewed.

Baptism is the primary ordination to discipleship and ministry. And all persons, both those we call "laity" and "ordained," are people of God. In fact, the Greek words for people of God are transliterated *laos theou*. *Laos* means "people"; *theou* is "of God." Our use of the word *laity* is itself rather narrow. Laity does not mean the uninitiated or the untrained. Rather, laity means the actual people of God, including also those we call "ordained," who through baptism are called, through the nurture and education of the Church are trained, and through continuing support in covenantal communities are supported in ministries of love and justice in the world. The word *ordination* also goes back to actions in the early Church of the "laying on of hands" to authorize a person's service as accountable to the Church. Through the bridge of the deacon, the partnership of the whole people of God, including those we have called laity and clergy, may be enhanced and shared—to build up the Church, to witness and nurture others, to study and interpret the meanings of the faith (do theology), and to serve and proclaim God's love and grace to all creation.

Rethinking the Church

Leonardo Boff's analysis that the Church is in a period of ecclesiogenesis, of renewal that gives new life and vocation to the Church, is accurate. Deacons in full connection not only have a servant ministry in the world; all deacons are also obligated to be on the pastoral staff of a congregation and be accountable to the ministry of a local church. In this way again, deacons embody, as do elders, that the Church's ministries are for the sake of the world, and that the realities of everyday life are brought into the Church for understanding, intercession, and care. Another way of expressing this reality is to say the Church "faces the world."[4] In this way, the Church faces into the world as a sailboat faces into the wind and the Church brings into its vision the faces of the world. As the Church faces the world, the Word of grace encountered in the incarnation of Jesus and the concrete realities of the world are engaged.

The image of "Body of Christ" communicates that the Church can only be the Church when the diverse gifts of the people of God are honored and shared. As deacons bridge and enliven the connection of Church and world, the body image is made concrete and real. A deacon who teaches health education and childcare to families in northern Mozambique extends the traditional definition of ordained minister. This deacon, as ordained minister, visits, checks on the health of children and family members, and brings the resources of healing and faith to families. In turn, the deacon brings to congregations the needs that inform the prayers of the people and that call all the people of God to ministries of visitation, health, and healing. As authorized and in the world, this ministry highlights how the vocations of other healthcare workers contribute to the world's health.

The Body of Christ becomes a reality. How the vocations of the people of God are honored and supported, how people of God work together in carrying out ministries and building up the world, and how acts of love, justice, and service witness to the reign of God breaking into the life of the world are the fundamental questions for the Church's life.

Moreover, a comparable image of the world is the place where Christ's body is lived, where Christ's blood is shed, and where Christ's life, commitment, and service are made real. The Church is in, but not of, the world. This classic statement of Christian theology is even truer today. The world is a place of amazing diversity of peoples and religious expressions. The world is broken by people's hatred in genocide, stereotyping, oppression, and war. The world does not teach in its everyday life the ministry of God. Of course, all people are children of God. Of course, people do see God's acts of hope, healing, transformation, and community in the midst of the world. Of course, God calls people to service and ministry through the particular realities of the world. Yet, to be faithful to this God we have met in Jesus, we need covenant groups filled with others who themselves are seeking faith, understanding, and vocation. We need others who will take our spiritual journey and our training for spiritual leadership and service seriously. We need education.

The new genesis of the Church is the empowering of persons through the ministries of support, conversation, study, and actions within covenantal communities seeking to build up the Body of Christ for love and service. Partnering with one another and with God in hearing the call, accepting the name "child of God," building up the Church, supporting one another on the journeys of faith, and serving in the name of Christ begin the new birth of the Church.

Duke Ellington, the great American jazz musician, nurtured in African American congregations, expressed his faith in his compositions. During World War II, one of his "sacred" works was "New World A-Comin'." In this work, he portrayed the power of God in bringing hope and new life to the struggle against racism. The composition was simultaneously a prayer and a proclamation pointing to God's presence calling the world.

Before it was performed in a 1966 concert on a cold winter night in France, Ellington introduced it with these words:

> The title refers to a future place, on earth, at sea or in the air where there will be no war, no greed, no categorization, and where love is unconditional, and where there is no pronoun good enough for God.[5]

This is a witness of a eucharistic model of ministry extending the table into the world participating in the mystery and life of Christ, finding nurture and sustenance in the life of the Body of Christ, and witnessing to the world of the promise of God to renew all creation and offer a great banquet.

Ministry is the Church offering to the world the grace, healing, love, and justice of God.

Rethinking Ordination

At the 1996 General Conference, the *Book of Discipline* was revised by expanding and highlighting the servant nature of all ministry. The ordained are called servant-leaders. The language hoped to communicate that all Christians are called to service and leadership.

They, in turn, limited the language of "representative minister," which had been found in earlier books of discipline, and used extensively in ecumenical conversation about the ordained. In 1982 in *Baptism, Eucharist and Ministry,* for example, the Faith and Order Commission of the World Council of Churches defined the ministry of the ordained and consecrated as representative in the following words:

> Ordained ministers are representatives of Jesus Christ to the community, and proclaim his message of reconciliation. As leaders and teachers they call the community to submit to the authority of Jesus Christ. . . . As pastors, under Jesus Christ the chief shepherd, they assemble and guide the dispersed people of God, in anticipation of the coming Kingdom.[6]

The authors of the United Methodist legislation for 1996, believing that all persons could represent Christ, removed "representative" as descriptor exclusively for the ordained. Children can represent Christ as they empathically reach out to another in love and service. Laity living faithfully their ministries in daily life are representing Christ.

Instead, in the *1996 Discipline,* ordination is defined as "a gift from God" (par. 303.1) whereby persons who show "evidence of God's grace, and promise of future usefulness are affirmed by the community, and who respond to God's call by offering themselves in leadership as ordained ministers" (par. 301.2). The ordained make commitments to "conscious living of the whole gospel" and its "proclamation . . . to the end that the world may be saved" (par. 303.1). In turn, the ordained lead the people through ministries of "Service, Word, Sacrament, and Order" (par. 303.2).

"Service is a primary representation of God's love" (par. 303.2). The emphasis on service and the servant leadership of both clergy and laity was an effort to undergird the ministry of the laity and the call of all Christians to mission in the name of the God we know in Christ. However, service and servant leadership do not avoid the limitations of the previous use of representative. All people of God are in service following Christ in witnessing and working for the good of creation. Servant leadership is open to both lay and ordained.

If we are not careful, we will counter the gains being made in mutuality and partnership that are occurring because of the rethinking of ministry and the Church. The use of service to designate the work of the ordained will have a tendency to restrict the notion of servanthood to the ordained—to the elder and the deacon. The language of ordination emphasizing Word, Sacrament, Order, and Service for elders and Word and Service for deacons does not adequately clarify ordination. The focus on servanthood for the ordained can have the effect of limiting rather than expanding the ministry of the people of God in the world. It also ignores the reality that the ordained themselves are *laos theou,* people of God, laity.

United Methodists have tended to act functionally and pragmatically. As we have reshaped our understandings of the ministry of the laity, of the deacon, and of the elder,

141

we have functioned pragmatically to extend the ministries of the Church and to enhance the connection between world and Church. In fact, in the early Church, just such a functional reality led people to be set apart for leadership, for embodying God's grace, and for being recognized by the Church. Yet, more than this was a concrete recognition that God was active in a person's life in unique ways.

Of course, we want to avoid the increased hierarchy that developed as ordained leaders of the Church paralleled the offices of leadership in the Roman government and social structure after the fifth century. In that hierarchy, the ordained were set apart from laity and seen as more holy. Then, in turn, bishops were ordained to a higher calling, and archbishops to an even higher calling.

Ordination does not mean one is more holy. Rather, ordination is the Church's authorization of a person to be "set apart" in his or her calling and to "stand for" the Church in his or her actions. Ordination is not being ordained to a role of servanthood. All Christians are called as servants. Ordination does not mean being ordained to leadership, for many laity lead in the world and congregations.

We need to think again about how we define ordination. One of the deacons we interviewed was angered at the tendency of some in her Annual Conference to see the title *deacon* as a recognition of a status and a fulfillment of training, rather than a calling. This tendency has been embedded in the Church from the beginning. It is a tendency we need to counter.

Let us suggest a fuller description of ordination. Ordination, theologically, is distinguished by three understandings: (1) continuity, (2) representative, and (3) sacrament.[7] Only as these three influence one another is a fulsome definition of ordination possible.

Continuity communicates connection over time. It stands for what has traditionally been termed *apostolic*.

142

One side of the definition of the word *apostolic* is the recognition that the Word of God is preached, that is, proclaimed to the community in word and deed. Those who proclaim this Word are apostles. Historically, just as the one who presides at the sacraments has been designated by Church action, the Church has recognized those who have gifts, inspired by the Holy Spirit, to faithfully proclaim the power of God's reign known in the incarnation of Christ. These persons have been officially authorized to proclaim the Word. Of course, even people who are not authorized proclaim the Word of redemption, new life, and God's reign, but the Church has particularly recognized and taken particular responsibility for some to be in continuity with the tradition and to proclaim the Word.

Representative means to re-present Christ to the world, to be a vehicle through which God's love and transformation are experienced. As we have mentioned, the word *representative* carries many meanings:

1. As a re-presentation—a person, the human and faulted vehicle, through which the Holy is encountered. (This view of representative is developed in *Baptism, Eucharist and Ministry.*)
2. As a representative—standing in the place of another and embodying the values and carrying the message of another. (This is the view that some fear will usurp the ministry of the laity.)
3. As representing another—as an elected "official," such as those elected to the House of Representatives in the United States Congress. These representatives are persons who felt drawn to leadership, who offered themselves for election, and who, for a period of time, have been chosen to consult and vote in fulfilling the tasks of legislation. In addition, in law, the word *represent* is used for the official person chosen to argue a case, a point of view, or a defense. The lawyer who represents a person is officially recognized as such even by the court.

143

A combination of these terms can fill out the meaning of the word *represent*. On the one hand, through deacons' ministries, people do encounter Christ. In addition, deacons' ministries seek to represent the Church in the world and the call and service of Christ. But even more, they, as is also true of elders, are ones authorized officially by the Church to represent it. Laity also represent Christ; they represent the Church too. However, the laity are not authorized as official spokespersons for the Church who are, in turn, particularly accountable to live out, defend, and advocate for the Church.

Finally, *sacramental* means that ordination is an official and acknowledged recognition of pointing to (making visible) God's presence in the world. Thereby, people come to see the presence of the Holy in the world. Many deacons with whom we spoke were surprised to learn that people who encountered them and their ministries thought of their work as sacramental. In a eucharistic model of ministry, through the sacrament, people encounter the grace of God and participate in the witness, renewal, and promise embedded in this "Great Banquet." Moreover, deacons "extend the table" and thus again provide conditions whereby persons encounter the grace of God and participate concretely in the witness, renewal, and promise of the "Great Banquet."

Ordination is the Church's official recognition of those from the laity *(laos theou)* called to proclaim, interpret, represent, empower, and provide sacrament. These persons have a particular responsibility in their lives. Their tasks are not better than those of other people of God who are also called through baptism to service and interpretation; rather they are recognized and authorized to speak on behalf of the Church. And, in turn, they have the covenantal responsibility to fulfill this task for the Church.

The Deacon's Heart

We began this book with the idea of a deacon's heart, describing a gathering of persons who shared their commitments to God's service. We have discovered and reported the ministries of persons who have deacons' hearts. They love God's creation, seek healing and justice, and work with others in partnership in the Church and in the world. They offer new options to the Church. They gather to support one another and to equip others for ministries of faithfulness.

Yet, even more, we have discovered the moment of opportunity and hope that has presented itself to the Church. The revision of the orders of ministry has opened all of us to new meanings for ministry, ordination, and partnership. The heart of a deacon, the heart of service, is extended into all the world through the love of God and the ministries of the Church.

We gather at table and celebrate the gracious love God continues to extend to creation. We are children of God, loved and forgiven. Through God's grace, we are called to extend our minds, our hearts, and our hands in God's service in the world.

Again and again, God reminds us who we are. Again and again, God loves us. Again and again, God calls and empowers us for ministry. May these stories be signs of God's love and justice. May these stories be proclamations of the life-giving word of God. May they give us all hope, strength, and vision as we seek to be God's Church to a hurting world.

NOTES

1. A Deacon's Heart

1. These research tools are called "ethnographic," that is, research grounded in the experiences and actions of people in community. Throughout this book we have identified the people we have interviewed by their first names or by pseudonyms. We have not listed all of the many Garrett-Evangelical students with whom we talked. We use their words and their ministries only with their permission. We believe that they need to be honored and respected as unique children of God with unique experiences and gifts.

2. An Abundance of Need

1. Interview with Bishop Joao Machado in Maputo, Mozambique, March 22, 1999.

2. *Deacons: Ministers of Justice and Charity*, video by the Roman Catholic Bishops' Committee on the Diaconate (Washington, D.C., 1998).

3. Ibid., quote from Deacon John Pistone.

4. From *The United Methodist Hymnal* #733 (Nashville: The United Methodist Publishing House, 1989).

5. *Deacons: Ministers of Justice and Charity*.

6. See Kenneth Rowe, "The Ministry of Deacons in Methodism from Wesley to Today," *Quarterly Review* 19 (winter 1999): 343-56.

7. Leonardo Boff, *Ecclesiogenesis: The Base Communities Reinvent the Church* (Maryknoll, N.Y.: Orbis Books, 1986).

8. Susan Wilhauck and Paul Van Buren, "The First United Methodist Deacons in Full-Connection: A Study of Diaconal Ministers Who Transitioned to the Order of Deacons" (report presented to The General Board of Higher Education and Ministry, The United Methodist Church, October 1998).

3. Called to Ministry, Authorized by the Church

1. Reta Finger, *Paul and the Roman House Churches* (Scottdale, Pa.: Herald Press, 1993).

2. Diedra Kriewald, "*Diakonia* as a 'Sacred Order' in The United Methodist Church," *Quarterly Review* 19 (winter 1999): 358.

3. Ibid.

4. Ibid., 362.

5. Ibid., 361.

6. Laceye Warner, "Wesley Deaconess-Evangelists: Exploring Remnants of Revivalism in Late 19th Century British Methodism," *Methodist History* 38 (April 2000): 176-90.

7. Ibid.

8. Ibid.

9. *Handmaidens of the Lord: Pentecostal Women Preachers and Traditional Religion* (Philadelphia: University of Pennsylvania Press and Publications of the American Folklore Society, 1988).

10. Candidates should check with their Annual Conference to determine what academic preparation will be acceptable.

11. The commissioned period lasts from three to six years with extension under special circumstances for an additional three years.

4. An Incarnational Vocation

1. "The Call to Service," *Pastoral Statement on the Permanent Diaconate* (autumn 1993): 6.

2. See also Diedra Kriewald's description of the appropriate use of vestments. "Diakonia as a 'Sacred Order' in The United Methodist Church," *Quarterly Review* 19 (winter 1999): 365-66.

5. The Ministry of the Deacon: Bridging and Empowering

1. For a discussion, see Thomas E. Frank, *Polity, Practice and the Mission of The United Methodist Church* (Nashville: Abingdon Press, 1997), p. 149.

2. Ibid.

3. Dwight W. Vogel and Linda J. Vogel, *Sacramental Living: Falling Stars* and *Coloring Outside the Lines* (Nashville: Upper Room Books, 1999), p. 24.

4. Bishop William B. Oden in his paper for Formation events, "The Ministry of the Deacon," p. 2.

5. In *Basin & Towel* 2 (summer 1999), a newsletter of the Section of Deacons and Diaconal Ministries, Division of Ordained Ministry, General Board of Higher Education and Ministry.

6. Frank, *Polity, Practice, and the Mission of The United Methodist Church*, p. 147.

7. Maria Harris, *Fashion Me a People: Curriculum in the Church* (Louisville: Westminster/John Knox Press, 1989), pp. 34-35.

6. The Order of Deacons: A Communal Identity

1. Survey conducted by Susan Wilhauck and the Division of Ordained Ministry, Section of Deacons and Diaconal Ministries, General Board of Higher Education and Ministry, 1999.

2. See Sondra Higgins Matthaei, *Making Disciples: Faith Formation in the Wesleyan Tradition* (Nashville: Abingdon Press, 2000).

3. These statements from orders are unpublished statements collected by the Section of Deacons and Diaconal Ministries, Division of Ordained Ministry, General Board of Higher Education and Ministry.

4. Description of the meeting of the Order of Deacons, Baltimore-Washington Conference, by the Rev. Patti Smith, Dean of the Order.

7. Partnership: Deacons, Elders, and Laity

1. Barbara Brown Taylor, *The Preaching Life* (Cambridge, Mass.: Cowley Publications, 1993), pp. 21-22.

2. Ibid., p. 23.

3. Ibid.

4. For creative work on ordination in The United Methodist Church, see Jack Harnish, *The Orders of Ministry in The United Methodist Church* (Nashville: Abingdon Press, 2000).

5. See Diedra Kriewald, "Diakonia as a 'Sacred Order' in The United Methodist Church," *Quarterly Review* 19 (winter 1999): 365-66.

8. Accountability, Appointments, and Benefits

1. The author is the former Assistant General Secretary, Section of Deacons and Diaconal Ministers, Division of Ordained Ministry General Board of Higher Education and Ministry of The United Methodist Church and is presently the Executive Director of the Southeastern Jurisdictional Administrative Council at Lake Junaluska, North Carolina. This chapter has been edited by the present Assistant General Secretary, Joaquín García.

2. See also *The Ministry Interpretation Handbook—2000* (Nashville: General Board of Higher Education and Ministry, 2000).

3. See *The Ministry Interpretation Handbook—2000.*

4. "IRS Issues Private Letter Ruling on Deacons" (press release from The General Council on Finance and Administration, The United Methodist Church, December 11, 1998).

9. Rethinking Ministry, Church, and Ordination in The United Methodist Church

1. Edward Farley, *The Fragility of Knowledge: Theological Education in the Church and the University* (Philadelphia: Fortress Press, 1988), p. 92.

2. See Sondra Higgins Matthaei, *Making Disciples: Faith Formation in the Wesleyan Tradition* (Nashville: Abingdon Press, 2000).

3. "The Call to Service," *Pastoral Statement on the Permanent Diaconate* (autumn 1993), p. 6.

4. See Jack L. Seymour, ed., *Mapping Christian Education: Approaches to Congregational Learning* (Nashville: Abingdon Press, 1997).

5. *Encore*, August 23-29, 1999, pp. 25, 27.

6. World Council of Churches, *Baptism, Eucharist and Ministry* (Geneva: World Council of Churches, 1982), p. 21.

7. For a helpful analysis of ordination in the Methodist tradition, see Jack Harnish, *The Orders of Ministry in The United Methodist Church* (Nashville: Abingdon Press, 2000).